CONTENTS

WHO IS THIS BOOK WRITTEN FOR?

The aim of the book is to illustrate how all teachers are responsible for encouraging and developing the language skills of their students. This cannot be left entirely to those who teach English. The book is intended, therefore, for those involved in the other Humanities subjects and in the Sciences, Technical, Business and Craft courses. Since encouraging and developing language skills is a continuing process, the book will be useful for teachers at any level from lower Secondary school through to A Level and BTEC, as well as for all those who are preparing to teach in any of the above mentioned areas.

For this reason, the examples used in the book have been drawn from a wide range of subject areas and from a variety of levels of learning. Some examples will, therefore, be specifically relevant to teachers in one subject area, and others relevant to those in another; however, all examples are sufficiently clear for an analogy to be made in other subjects than those to which they specifically refer, and at other levels.

Because the intended readership is so wide, the term 'teacher' is used throughout the book to include lecturers, tutors, teachers and trainers. Similarly, the term 'student' is used to include pupils, students, trainees and clients.

Tasks

Throughout the book there are various tasks which illustrate some of the points made and provide an opportunity to apply these to the use and development of language skills. These tasks can be done by individuals working on their own but would be of more value if done in small groups. The book is an ideal vehicle for in-service training in subject departments, or throughout an educational establishment or training centre.

The tasks can also be performed by students, including those on constructing and evaluating materials. Because students are the main consumers in the education system, their evaluation of methods and materials is essential.

At the back of the book there is a selection of materials which can be used with the tasks. It is not essential to use these materials and some people may prefer to select their own which are more relevant to the subject and level that they teach. When doing this, however, we recommend that teachers use the examples at the back of the book to give an indication of the purpose of the task.

Scripts

The scripts are for use alongside a number of the tasks. For best results we recommend that teachers record these onto a tape.

Checklists

There are several checklists at various stages of the book which summarise the main points which need to be remembered when planning a scheme of work.

Photocopying

All the task pages, checklists, scripts and keypoint questions may be photocopied for educational purposes, but otherwise none of the materials in this book may be copied without the authorisation of the publishers.

INTRODUCTION

The main task of teachers is to develop students' knowledge in the specific areas of study that they have chosen. In order to do this, teachers not only need to develop students' practical skills; they also need to develop the language skills that accompany them. There are new words to learn, familiar words take on new meanings, new forms of reading materials are encountered, various ways of recording information and new styles of writing need to be mastered. Those who succeed in acquiring these language skills are most likely to succeed on their course.

Many students cope with this learning process, or they possess already many of these language skills. However, those in schools, colleges and training agencies with lower levels of language skills will find it hard even on the most basic courses. The immediate task, therefore, is to find ways to improve these students' language skills so that they too can succeed.

Students learn the language of their course by experiencing it and experimenting with it. Their competence grows through an interaction of writing, talking, listening, reading and experience. Yet this development cannot always be left to chance; it occasionally has to be supported by explicit instruction. Students need to be taught new vocabulary, its use, meaning and spelling. They must learn the appropriate ways of recording information and how this should be passed on either orally or in writing. They need to know where to look for information and they need to develop their ability to express themselves orally and in writing.

The development of all these language skills cannot be a discrete skill to be taught in isolation. It must primarily be part of the students' general development within their course. Because the language evolves in conjunction with the acquisition of knowledge in the subject, it is better that the students are taught the language skills as they occur in the classroom or workshop. Explicit instruction within a context is of more value since the students see it as relevant and are therefore more likely to remember it.

Teachers are not, therefore, solely concerned with teaching specific subject skills; they must also develop the language skills of their students.

This book illustrates, in a practical way, how the various language skills can be developed as an integral part of the teaching of any subject. It is set out as a progression from one skill to another and in such a way that students can gradually build up their competence. Whilst it is preferable to deal with each of the skills in the same order that they occur in the book, this may not always be necessary or practicable. Some skills may not be needed. You may not have control over the design of the course, and skills which occur towards the end of the book might have to be used at the beginning of your course. Sometimes, the period of study may be too short to deal adequately with all the skills, and it may be better to select and concentrate on those which are of most importance. But if you are able to determine how your course is structured and you have sufficient time, then it is recommended that all the skills are integrated in the order they occur in the book.

We have not included all aspects of developing language skills here. The book is mainly intended for those who are not specialists in English language teaching. (This does not mean it has nothing to say to the English teacher; it has.) For this reason, the book does not investigate any of the theories of language skills acquisition or the physiological and psychological aspects of language and learning. Other books do this adequately and for those whose interest is aroused, we give a short list of books in the Bibliography.

A technical or vocational teacher is an expert in his or her own field; he or she cannot be expected to deal with all the problems that arise in language skills acquisition. Where students show signs of having extensive problems, then the teacher must refer the student to whatever expertise exists within his or her establishment. I would not want to discourage teachers from taking an interest in the role of language development and learning and trying to find out as much as possible about it, but I would not recommend that they try to supplant those who have the time, the resources and the expertise.

Curriculum and resources development

When students attend a school or enrol on a course at a college or training agency, it is unlikely that they will be taught by the same person all the time. Within a department or establishment, therefore, there will need to be some liaison and co-operation on how the language skills are to be integrated into the main coursework. Most establishments have regular meetings at which curriculum issues are discussed, and the integration of language skills can be added to the agenda. It is essential that staff are given time for this liaison, not only at the beginning of a course or academic year but on a regular basis. This liaison has many benefits both for the staff and for the students. It allows staff to devise and develop methods and materials collectively so that there is consistency in their approach to teaching a language skill. It avoids duplication on the introduction of a skill and ensures that once a skill has been learned, it can be reinforced in a variety of situations. It allows for constant evaluation so that methods and materials can be revised and the roles of the teachers in the learning process can be renegotiated if necessary.

These regular meetings will obviously generate a lot of ideas and materials which need to be recorded and stored in an easily accessible resources bank for use by all the staff. The resources bank should try to include as wide a range of materials as possible, and staff should be aware of their existence and of how they can be used. It is better if the responsibility for compiling the resources and advising staff on their use is given to one or two people, preferably with some specialist knowledge on language skills.

Whether the resources are overseen by a specialist or not, they should include some books on the theories of language skills acquisition and the physiological and psychological aspects of language and learning. Other books ought to be included which give practical guidance on the basic skills of spelling, punctuation and grammar.

There are also an increasing number of books which, though designed originally for teaching vocational and academic English to speakers of other languages, do provide useful materials and exercises which are suitable for English native speakers. Some of the more general books are listed in the Bibliography, but there are others which deal with specific vocational and academic subjects such as catering, computers and IT, tourism and engineering.

The resources will naturally include a range of worksheets which have been devised by the teaching staff. Suggestions on what sheets might be useful are given throughout the book. These will include listening and reading tasks at a variety of levels with some preparatory materials and extended tasks to accommodate the mixed range of abilities of students. The worksheets will not only be available for use by staff but can act as models for developing new materials.

There should also be a range of handouts, articles and leaflets with information that can be used to promote discussion, role play and for project work. These should be from a variety of sources and at a variety of levels so that any one topic will have material which can be used and understood by any student. Other materials can be included in a resource bank such as cassette tapes, videos, slides, wall charts, OHP transparencies, etc., etc.

Of course, having such a wealth of resources is not much use unless there is quick and easy access. It will be necessary, therefore, to devise some form of catalogue system. A file should be kept with separate entries for each of the language skills (see the list on pages 8 and 9). Under each of the entries a list can be made of all the materials in the resource bank that deal with that skill. The list can also be graded with an indication of whether particular material is suitable for basic, intermediate or advanced work. The terminology used and how these are differentiated will depend on the type of course. Separate files can also be drawn up for different topics or themes or related to the sequence of the coursework. Building a resources bank and cataloguing it can be time-consuming at first, but it makes life much easier later.

Finding the level

Most courses include a large variety of language skills, and the first step will be to identify these. Students are sometimes expected to use more advanced skills than they really need for their course.

It is, therefore, not simply a case of identifying which language skills are used, but also of determining what level is appropriate. This will depend on what the students need to complete their course and enter employment or higher education.

Most course books nowadays, such as those for CPVE, GCSE and BTEC, are designed and written for students at that particular ability level, and a great deal of care is taken to ensure that the layout and language used is suitable. Unfortunately, this is not always the case; some books try to appeal to a wide range of people, CPVE and A level students, novices and experts. Though some of the information contained in these books is needed for the lower level student, it is often set out and written in a style more suitable for the higher level student. Similarly, where course books are not available, teachers have to use other materials. Here again, the information will be relevant but will have been written for a wider audience, and consequently the language and layout used might be at an inappropriate level.

Teaching materials, therefore, need to be carefully selected or adapted to suit the ability of the students they are intended for. Students with lower levels of language ability are often capable of meeting the requirements of their course but struggle because the materials are inappropriate. For these students to cope, they need to be given a careful introduction to the language of their course and guidance on how it is used.

Teaching styles and methods also need to be adapted to suit the ability level of the students. Some students can adequately understand how a process works by reading about it or listening to a lecture. Others need to see the process demonstrated, and others need the experience of doing it themselves. But at any of these levels, if the language used and the manner in which it is explained is not appropriate, then the students will experience difficulty.

To assess the skills and levels of a course that you teach, look at the checklist on pages 8 to 10.

Checklist ASSESSING THE SKILLS AND LEVELS OF A COURSE

1 Think of a group of students that you teach.

2 Look through the list of language skills below and on the next page.
   a) What skills do students need in your class? Put a tick in column 1.
   b) If there are any extra skills, add these to the list.
   c) For each of the skills that you have identified, work through the flow chart on page 10.
   d) If you decide that action needs to be taken on any of these skills, put a tick in column 2 of the language skills list.

3 Now consult colleagues who teach the same students and get them to go through the list and chart in the same way that you have.

   Where you have both identified skills on which action needs to be taken, then you will need to liaise on how methods and materials need to be changed.

   If students need guidance, then you will have to devise a strategy with the other staff on how skills are to be introduced and/or reinforced.

   If there is disagreement over the level of ability of the students and the need for guidance, then you will need to discuss this. Are your expectations too high or low? Are the methods and materials that you use appropriate? Is there consistency between different teachers?

4 If you are the only member of staff who teaches the students, then you will have to resolve these issues yourself though advice should be sought from colleagues where possible.

Reading
Do the students have to read
– textbooks
– manuals
– handouts
– worksheets
– blackboards/OHPs
– commercially produced leaflets
– packages of materials

Column 1 required of students? √/X	Column 2 action required? √/X

Writing
Do the students need to
– make notes from textbooks
– make notes from a lecture
– write essays
– copy from a blackboard/OHP
– write reports
– do written projects/assignments

Language Guidelines © 1990 ALBSU. Published by Hodder & Stoughton.

	Column 1 required of students? √/X	Column 2 action required? √/X

Reference skills
Do the students need to
– look things up in textbooks/manuals/
  catalogues, etc.
– refer to their notes
– pick out information from a text

Oral/aural skills
Do the students have to
– take dictation
– answer questions orally
– ask for information
– participate in role play
– participate in discussions
– give talks

Graphic materials
Do the students need to understand
– diagrams
– charts
– maps
– graphs
– tables

Testing
What forms of testing are used?
– multiple choice
– one word answers
– single sentence answers
– single paragraph answers
– essays
– completing graphs/charts/diagrams, etc.

Analysis of teaching methods and materials

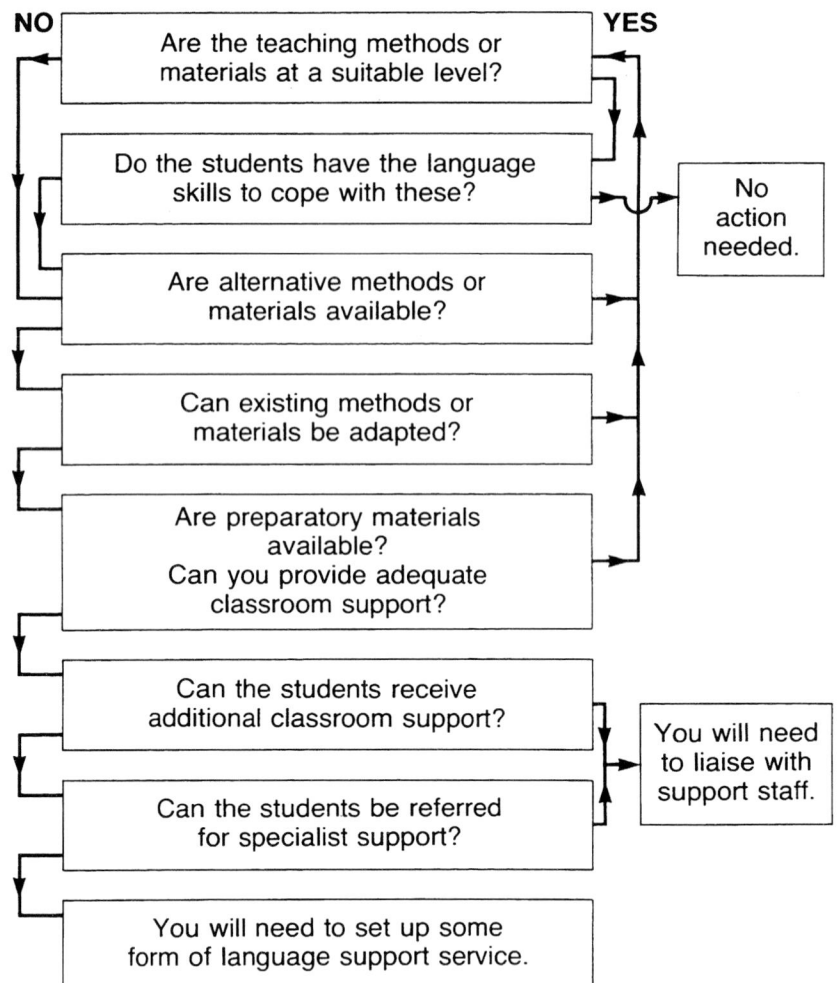

READING

INTRODUCTION

Most text books, manuals and technical journals fall into the difficult end of the spectrum when measured for **readability** (how easy or difficult they are to read). Even students who have a high level of reading ability may find difficulty in coping with some of the reading materials they use on their course. This is a significant handicap, especially as many courses are now changing to assignment and project work which require students to research materials independently. Even if assignments and projects are not required, however, reading is still a substantial part of most courses and usually occurs away from the classroom or workshop. It is, therefore, important that students are adequately prepared for their reading.

Preparing students for their reading

- Make sure that students understand the vocabulary they are likely to come across: not only the technical terms for tools, machinery and processes, but also conceptual terms like 'expansion', 'composition', 'equivalent' and words which have subject-specific meanings different from their normal usage, like 'bed', 'neck', 'skirt'.
- Help students establish a purpose to their reading by identifying the key pieces of information they are looking for in their reading.
- Help students analyse texts and extract the key points.
- Make sure students know where to look for information and how to extract it quickly and accurately.
- Having introduced all these aspects, reinforce them in a variety of ways: discussion, writing and alternative reading materials.

ASSESSING STUDENTS' LANGUAGE SKILLS

We need to know the abilities and reading levels of the students before we can decide on the appropriateness of reading materials and the strategies we need to employ to encourage and develop reading skills.

In most secondary schools, the curriculum will indicate what language skills have been developed and at what level, as the students progress through the school. There will also be some form of assessment to show whether a student has managed to acquire those skills and achieved the appropriate level adequately. Secondary school teachers, therefore, will have a record of the abilities and reading levels of the students who arrive in their classrooms at the beginning of the academic year.

Teachers in FE colleges and training agencies, however, cannot refer to the student's school records (and in many cases these would be of limited use, since the student is re-entering learning after an absence of several years). These teachers, therefore, require some way of making an assessment of a student's language skills and reading level.

It is possible to assess a student's language ability from a short test administered at the beginning of a course. Although the test will primarily be assessing the student's ability to read and understand a text, it can be a fairly reliable guide to show which students will have problems with other language skills. Since the period of attendance by a student at an FE college or training agency is relatively short, teachers need to know immediately what materials are going to be appropriate and what language skills need to be developed. A re-appraisal can be made later, but experience has shown that a well constructed test is a good general indicator of a student's overall language ability.

Not many commercially produced tests are available for students in upper secondary schools, colleges or adult education but here are three ready-made tests which could be used.

Gapadol Test

This is a short, simple test consisting of six cloze passages of various types of prose and degrees of difficulty. A cloze passage is one in which words are left out and the student has to decide what the missing words are by reading the passage. Words are missed out on a systematic basis. It may be that every ninth word is omitted or every eighth or seventh word. The Gapadol test is easy to mark, and the score can be translated into a reading age. The greater the number of words which are correctly guessed, the higher the reading age. The reading age is graded from 10 years and below through to 16 years and above. The interpretation of the raw score as a reading age needs to be handled with care, since reading age is sometimes (erroneously) equated with mental age, and can have a detrimental effect on students.

Some people might think that the Gapadol test is too short and simple and does not examine a student's ability in any detail. However, being subjected to a substantial test at the beginning of a course can be very intimidating for some students, particularly if they have been out of education for a long time. It may only be necessary to make a general evaluation of ability at first and a more detailed investigation can be made when each of the relevant language skills is encountered in later work. All that the teacher needs initially is a guide for the level of approach to those skills.

There is also the problem that the passages are not appropriate or relevant to the course that the student is studying. Whether a student who is doing a motor vehicle course can read and understand a description of a person in a literary style may not be regarded as essential. Using a general test will, however, give an indication of which students may need additional support to cope with the language skills on their course. Having identified these students, an evaluation can follow later on an individual basis which is more relevant to their particular course.

■ The Gapadol Test can be obtained from Heinemann Educational Books, Halley Court, Jordan Hill, Oxford OX2 8EJ.

Edinburgh Reading Test: Stage 4

This is a more substantial test which splits language skills into five sections and tests each of them individually (skimming, vocabulary, reading for fact, point of view, comprehension). The test takes longer to administer and score than the Gapadol test but obviously provides a better indication of the student's ability. A profile can be drawn up to show the strengths and weaknesses of the student. The exercises are on various topics and vary in difficulty.

There is the same problem about relevance with this test as there is in the Gapadol test and, since this is more substantial, it may be inappropriate for students who are pursuing a specific subject. However, such courses may include a variety of language skills, and until the students have learned something about the subject, the question of relevance may not arise. The skill of reading often requires some knowledge of the subject being discussed, e.g. vocabulary and concepts. Unless students have that knowledge, they will have problems, not because their reading ability is low, but because they do not know the subject well enough. It is clear that the motor vehicle students will respond more positively to a test which mentions motor vehicles and related topics, and that this will give a more accurate assessment of how they will respond to the language needs of the course.

As with the Gapadol test, the scores can be translated to a reading age and so the comments made earlier also apply here.

■ The Edinburgh Reading Test can be obtained from Hodder and Stoughton Publishers, Mill Road, Dunton Green, Sevenoaks, Kent TN13 2YA.

Assessing Reading (ALBSU)

As with the Gapadol test, this is a series of cloze passage of various type of prose and degrees of difficulty. However, unlike the Gapadol test, the passages can be selected and administered according to their perceived appropriateness. The topics of many of the passages relate to specific vocational subjects such as catering, hairdressing, construction, retailing and motor vehicles. If none of these is thought appropriate, guidance is given in an accompanying booklet on how to construct your own passage.

The tests are all easy to administer and score and, unlike the previous two tests, are not translated into reading ages. The tests are useful initial indicators of those students who may need additional support in coping with language skills, and the pack of materials is flexible enough to be used in any situation.

When constructing your own tests, the pack illustrates how to assess the difficulty of a text by using a special formula known as the SMOG formula. (The Flesch test, which is explained in the next part, can be used and is equally appropriate.) Having assessed the difficulty of the passage, the ability of the student can be measured by the number of words that they can supply correctly.

- More than 60% right – they can read material at this level with understanding.
- Between 40% and 60% – they will need some support to cope with materials at this level.
- Less than 40% right – they cannot read material at this level adequately; other materials will have to be devised or selected at a simpler level.

- The Assessing Reading Test is available from the Adult Literacy and Basic Skills Unit, Kingsbourne House, 229–231 High Holborn, London WC1V 7DA.

ASSESSING MATERIALS

Most courses start with an introductory text book which is supplemented with other materials such as teacher-produced handouts, magazine and newspaper articles, etc. The teacher usually has control of when the students read these, so initially it is possible to select reading materials and ensure that students are adequately prepared before they read. This initial preparation will ensure that students are then able to cope more effectively with other texts which they will select as independent readers.

There are objective ways of assessing reading materials but these cannot be the sole criteria for assessing how easy or difficult a text is to read. Neither do they indicate what features make a text more difficult or how students can be prepared. However, they are a quick, objective method of assessing materials and can serve as a useful starting point.

The Flesch Test

The 'Flesch' test is one of several methods that have been devised to try to indicate the readability of written materials, i.e. how difficult or easy something is to read.

To work out a score, use the following formula:

- Count 100 words of continuous prose from a text.
- Count how many syllables there are in these 100 words.
- Calculate the average number of words per sentence in these 100 words.
- Score = 206.835
    minus (0.846 × number of syllables)
    minus (1.015 × number of words per sentence)

The higher the resulting score, the simpler the text.

Notes for calculations

- A word is a set of letters or characters which is delimited by a space at either end. Hyphenated words, numbers, abbreviations and acronyms are all counted as one word, e.g. father-in-law, 1989, BBC, NALGO.

- A syllable is harder to define so you will have to rely on your own pronunciation as to whether such words as 'diary' contain two or three syllables. Numbers and abbreviations, however, are counted as one syllable but acronyms, such as NALGO, count as two syllables.

Quick calculation of Flesch score

A quicker but slightly less accurate method is to use a ruler between the left and right hand columns of the chart on the opposite page.

Move the left hand side of the ruler until the top edge corresponds with the number of words per sentence. Now move the right hand side of the ruler until the top edge corresponds to the number of syllables. Where the ruler crosses the centre column will give you an indication of the level of difficulty.

For example, a passage with 5 sentences (or 20 words per sentence) and 155 syllables gives a reading of approximately 55.5 which means it is fairly difficult to read.

T A S K

Using the Flesch formula, calculate the readability of several different passages.
Think about why each score is obtained (is it the length of the sentences, the length of the words, or both?).
Think about whom each passage was written for and whether it is at an appropriate level.

TASK SHEET: 1

Other Factors Influencing Readability

The sole premise of the Flesch Test (and others like it) is that if a piece of writing has long sentences and long words, it will be difficult to read or that, conversely, if it has short sentences and short words, it will be easy to read. This is no doubt true, but there are other things that need to be taken into consideration.

One consideration is how much the content of the piece fits in with the reader's existing knowledge. Passage A (on task sheet 1) has a high score, since it was written for young children and should theoretically be easy to read, but it does require a basic knowledge of the concepts of mass and atmosphere. Passage C, which was written for the 'layperson', also scores high. A *Guardian* reader should understand the concepts of vertical and horizontal but may have difficulty with the technical terms 'head', 'stud' and 'plate'. Here they relate to things which are different from their common meaning. The writer might have expected that those who needed to read the article closely would have some knowledge of building terms.

Flesch chart

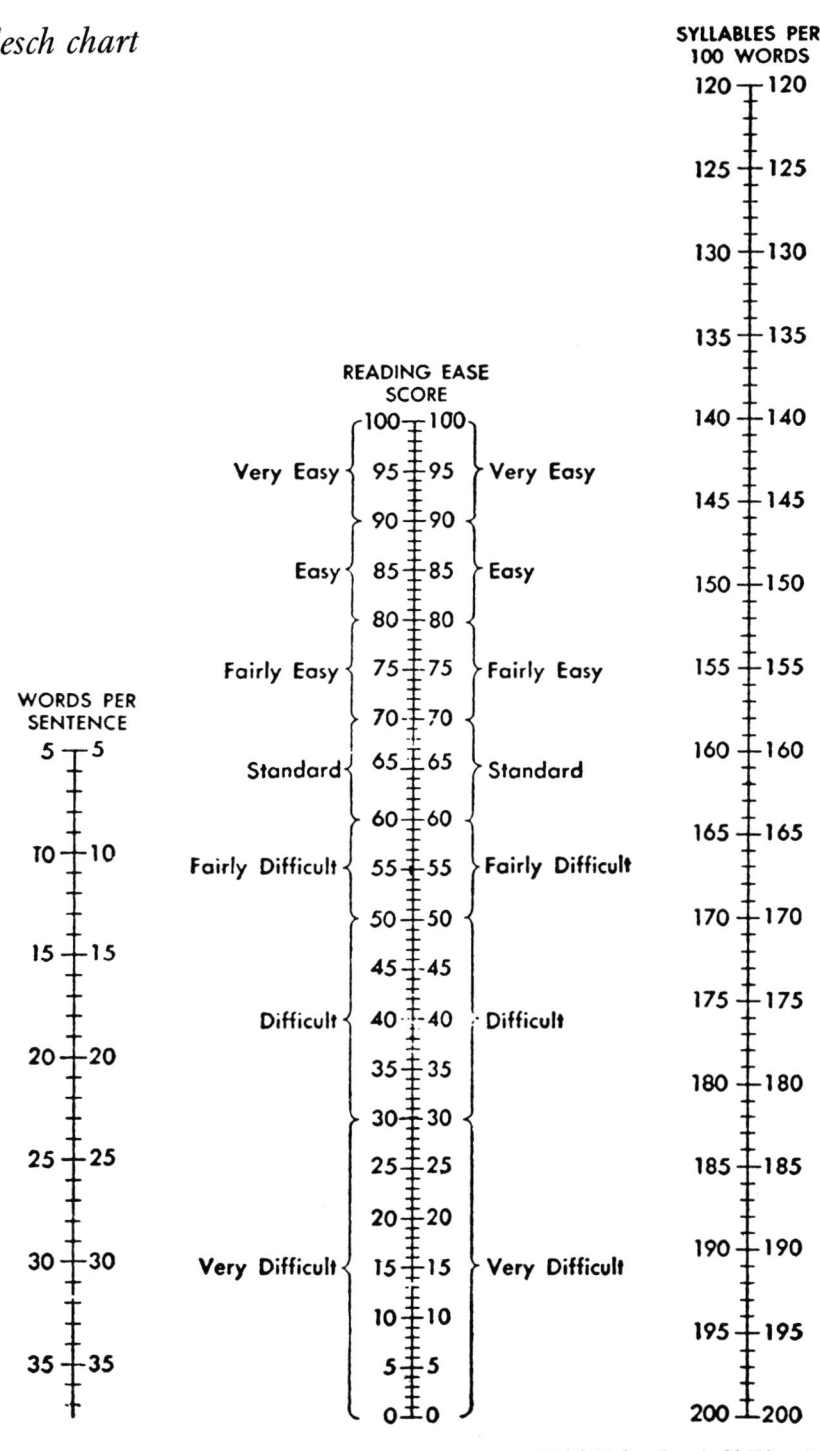

Another consideration is the style of language used and how complex the sentence structure is. Passage A is a simple description of a process which confines itself to one statement of fact per sentence. Passage D is also a simple description, but each sentence contains more than one statement of fact. It is possible to identify what each of these facts is without making too many changes to the wording (or even understanding what the facts are). For example, the first sentence contains the facts: nicotine is a drug; nicotine affects the nervous system; nicotine affects the circulatory system. The language style and sentence structure of Passage B, however, are much more complex: to simplify it you would need a deeper understanding of what the passage is about.

1 If a piece of writing does have a low score on the Flesch Test, i.e. it is difficult to read, make a list of the words that have three or more syllables. Then ask yourself:

a) Does the piece explain the meaning of the word?

e.g. A *malleable* material is one that can be hammered into thin sheets or small bars without cracking.

b) Are there any of those words with which the students are already familiar?

c) Can the meaning be guessed from the context of the piece?

e.g. A sky dappled with light, white *cirrocumulus* in the early morning generally leads to a fine, warm day.

d) Do the students have access to a dictionary or glossary where they can look up the meaning of the words? (It may be useful for students to compile their own dictionary or glossary during their course.)

2 If you have gone through the checklist and still have several words left on your list, you should consider whether it would be worthwhile asking your students to read the piece. It is no use asking them to read something if they are not going to be able to understand it. But if you still think that it is worthwhile reading matter, then prepare your students by checking that they know the meanings of words from your list **before** they have to read.

3 This same procedure should be applied to abbreviations and to words which have a different meaning from their common meaning.

e.g. The major source of *TVP* is the soya bean.

Each cashier is given a £20 *float*.

In computers, a programming mistake or error is called a *bug*.

Re your letter of the 23rd *inst*.

 Language Guidelines © 1990 ALBSU. Published by Hodder & Stoughton.

Long sentences can be difficult to understand, because they put a great load on short term memory and the capacity to process information. Sentence length and vocabulary are not, however, the only things that determine ease or difficulty. A text can be difficult if it uses complex structures or is written in a particular style. We have listed below styles of writing that create problems. It is obviously not wrong to use these, but you need to be aware of which type of language may create reading problems for students. Many of the features listed below occur in academic and technical texts which tend to be written in a formal style in order to give them greater objectivity. The degree of difficulty will depend on how familiar students are with the structure and style. The more exposure students get to these types of text then the easier they will find it to read them.

The Passive Voice

The passive voice causes difficulty because we tend not to use it in our everyday conversation, and because it often removes the 'human interest'.

e.g.   The apparatus was assembled.
        The ingredients were mixed.
        The mixture is ignited by a spark.
        First of all, the letters are delivered to the Mail Room.

The active voice is easier to understand, but it can make the sentence less formal and less objective.

e.g.   We assembled the apparatus.
        I mixed the ingredients.
        The spark ignites the mixture.
        First of all, you deliver the letters to the Mail Room.

Vagueness

It is harder for students to understand a text if it contains a lot of 'probability' or 'indeterminate' words.

e.g.   may, might, could, should
        rather, few, very, more or less, some
        usually, possibly, sometimes, often

Use of these words introduces a sense of abstraction into a text which makes it harder to relate to than a concrete reality. However, it is often difficult to avoid these types of words when they are used in passages concerned with probability and uncertainty.

e.g.   Several facts have led many investigators to suggest that the pyramids could have been constructed with the help of an ancient computer or perhaps by some visitors from outer space.

Clauses

A simple sentence is one that contains one main clause.

e.g.   Electricity has dramatically altered our way of life.

More clauses can be added, which then extend the information given in the sentence. Obviously, the more clauses that are used, the more complex the sentence becomes, because it involves retaining more information in short term memory to tie in with information given later in the sentence. It also makes it harder to follow the main 'thread' of the information being given in the sentence.

e.g.   Scope for more effective and less man-power intensive

1 Content

a) Is the subject matter interesting?

b) Is the subject matter relevant?

c) Do the students need to read it – is there a definite purpose?

d) Are there any concepts that the students may not understand?

All these factors will affect students' motivation for reading and how carefully they will read.

2 Format

a) Does the size of type make it hard to read?

(Type sizes are given in terms of point size; one point is equal to 1/72 of an inch. The size is taken from the top of such letters as 'b' to the bottom of such letters as 'g'.)

This is an example of 11 point. This is recommended as being the optimal size of type for ease and speed of reading with adult readers.

b) Are lower case or upper case letters used?

THIS IS AN EXAMPLE OF UPPER CASE TYPE (I.E. USING CAPITAL LETTERS ONLY). MOST PEOPLE DISLIKE READING UPPER CASE AND READ IT MORE SLOWLY. FLUENT READERS USE OVERALL WORD SHAPE AS A CUE, AND THUS A LINE OF UPPER CASE PRINT CONTAINS FOR THEM LESS INFORMATION THAN ONE WHICH HAS THE ASCENDERS AND DESCENDERS OF LOWER CASE TYPE.

c) Is the text accompanied by useful and suitable illustrations?

The size and style of type can affect the ease with which students can read. Illustrations can aid meaning and often break up long, complicated passages of text.

3 Organisation

a) Is the text set out in short paragraphs with spaces between?

b) Is the information given in meaningful sequences that are easy to follow?

c) Is the text broken up with suitable headings and sub-headings?

d) Is important information highlighted in boxes or by using different styles of type?

e) Is too much textual information crammed onto one page?

f) Are any summaries included in the text?

All these factors make it easier for students to extract information from a text – they can quickly pick out the sections they need to read and avoid wasting time reading those that they do not.

4 Style

a) What vocabulary is used – are there lots of long or unfamiliar words?

b) Are there lots of long sentences?

c) Is the style of language too formal or academic – are students familiar with this style of language?

These factors have already been discussed in the section on measuring readability. The less complicated the language, the easier it will be for students to understand.

Language Guidelines © 1990 ALBSU. Published by Hodder & Stoughton.

information exchange and business interaction was widened as the nineteenth century progressed by, first, the introduction of commercial telegraph services which linked most major towns and cities in Europe and North America by the 1870s as well as providing a transatlantic link in 1866, and, secondly, by the introduction of typewriters, which were initially mechanical but eventually converted to electronic operation during the 1920s.

Nominalisation

This is when a verb is turned into a noun. For example,
> If you reduce the length of string you will increase the speed of the pendulum

is easier to understand than:
> A reduction in the length of string will produce an increase in the speed of the pendulum.

Nominalisation, like the passive voice, takes out the human interest. It makes the sentence more abstract and difficult to relate to.
Another example (the nominalised verbs are in italics):
> Robots remove the components and deliver them to the production line

is easier than:
> The *removal* and *delivery* of the components to the production line is performed by robots.

TASK

Using the Flesch Test, the Vocabulary Checklist and Assessment Checklist, analyse the passages from two books and assess them for content, format, organisation and style.

TASK SHEETS: 2, 2a, 3, 3a

ENCOURAGING AND DEVELOPING READING SKILLS

Of course, reading materials should not be restricted to the level which had suited the students' ability at the beginning of their course. Eventually they will be expected to read an increasingly wide range of manuals, reports, reference books, etc., which will be written in a variety of particular styles that use certain technical words and terms. It is, therefore, essential that students should be encouraged to develop reading skills so that they will be able to read independently. They should also know where to look for information and how to extract what they need to know, easily and accurately.

Active Reading Exercises

Students should be encouraged to become active readers, i.e. they should be **doing** something while they are reading. They should be aware of the purpose of their reading and what information they are hoping to extract from a text. Active reading exercises are useful indicators that students have read and understood a particular text and they provide practice in using the language of the subject being studied.

There are several ways in which students can be encouraged to be active readers and to develop their reading skills. These are also useful in preparing students for written work, since it helps them to understand how a piece of writing should be organised and the sort of information that ought to be included in various types of text.

Initially, students should be given simple exercises which require little input from them; gradually the amount of input from them should be increased.

TASK

> Look at the examples of worksheets which include active reading exercises. These are:
> - filling in gaps
> - multiple choice questions
> - true/false statements
> - completing lists
> - filling in charts
> - labelling diagrams
>
> Complete the worksheets. Before looking through each of the texts, however, try to provide the answers from what you already know about the topic or make a considered guess of what the answers might be. Then read the text to see if you are right.
>
> *TASK SHEETS: 4, 5, 6, 7, 8*

When devising this type of exercise, try to ensure that the students are not merely copying out information directly from the text. The exercises should be designed to find out whether the students have understood the text and force them to think about what they are reading. Try to ensure that in completing the worksheet, the students are identifying key points of information.

Asking the students to answer the questions before reading the text helps them to think about what they already know. They then confirm whether this is correct or assimilate new knowledge into their existing knowledge with greater effect. When these exercises are completed, they often provide useful notes for revision, reference or extended writing. It is imperative, therefore, that at the initial stages, when student input is minimal, the exercises should provide good models.

Certain texts lend themselves to particular forms of note-taking. Though exercises which involve gap filling, multiple choice and true/false statements could be used for all texts, completing lists, charts and diagrams are only appropriate for some (see the chart on page 49 in the section on Writing).

Examples of the different forms of note making can be found on task sheets 32, 32a and 32b.

Keypoint Questions

Active reading exercises are useful as an initial phase in getting students to pick out essential information (keypoints) from a text, but eventually they should be able to extract this information independently without having to complete worksheets. In order to do this, they have to be aware of what key information they are likely to find in the different types of text that they come across. They must know, before reading, what they expect to learn from the text. As independent readers they have to establish their own purpose for reading a text.

There are several distinct types of text that your students are likely to read for their course. Obviously, these will not always be independent of one another and one type of text may contain elements of another. The main types of text can be distinguished as:

Narrative – this includes such things as biographies; what individuals did over long or short periods; reports of extended activities; descriptions of events.

Description of structure or mechanism – describing an object, machine or organism.

Description of process – detailing how something is done – this is more impersonal than instruction and, unlike narrative, they are actions which are usually repeated.

Instructions – these tell someone what action to take for preparing, making, repairing something; how to conduct themselves.

Classification – how things are ordered in different groups and what similarities or differences determine which group they belong to.

Exemplifying – a statement of a general rule or principle with illustrations of how it is applied; a general statement of fact or opinion with examples that support it.

Cause/Effect – why something happens or happened; the effect something can have.

Advantages/Disadvantages – detailing the advantages and disadvantages of systems, processes, equipment, machinery, etc.

Theme – information of various sorts is given about a specific subject; this text type tries to cover descriptions not covered by the other types but the text does not have to confine itself purely to description.

It is not only useful for students to be aware of these different types of text but also the sort of information that they contain. To do this they need to draw up a keypoint checklist. The checklist not only gives them questions to ask when they are reading a text, but also provides them with guidance on what information they ought to include when they do their own writing.

A selection of questions for each of the main types of text is included at the back of the book (see page 126). These are not definitive lists. There may be other questions which can be added from your lists and others will no doubt crop up later. Keep adding to the lists. There will never be an occasion when all the questions from a list can be answered by one text. It may be that certain bits of information do not apply to a particular case or they may not be regarded as essential information.

TASK

For each of the main types of text, listed on the previous page, draw up a list of questions that you feel might be answered by the sort of information that is usually included in this type of text.

e.g.   Description of a structure – what size is it?
                                    – what shape is it?
                                    – what is it made of?

When you have drawn up your list of questions, look through a variety of texts and identify which type of text each one is. Take your list of questions that relate to that type of text. If you know anything about the subject in the text, try to answer your questions.

Now read the text, filling in the answers to your questions or checking those answers you already have.

Is there any extra information in the text – could you draw up a general question to cover this?

Are there any unanswered questions from your list – is there a reason for this – could you find the information elsewhere?

TASK SHEETS: 4–12

Non-Textual Materials

Not all the information that students need to find will be in the form of written text. Sometimes, information will be supplied in diagrams, charts and tables. Often this form of presentation is more convenient and accessible to students, but some guidance and practice on extracting information may be needed. This can be dealt with in a similar way to that used for written texts through active reading exercises and keypoint questions; alternatively exercises like those on task pages 13, 14 and 14a can be devised to introduce students to symbolic and tabular presentation.

Sometimes, diagrams may be set out symbolically. Make sure that students know what all the symbols are but don't just give them a list of symbols and their meanings, incorporate an exercise so that they have to use the list.

TASK

Look at the examples of handouts on the task sheets listed below and, using these as a guide, devise your own worksheets.

TASK SHEETS: 13, 14, 14a

Remember that the exercises should not merely involve copying out information and ensure that the exercises concentrate on the key elements.

1 Make diagrams, graphs and charts simple — don't try to include too much information.

2 It is better to use several diagrams, charts, etc., than to try to fit too much information into one.

3 Make sure all the labelling is clear and large enough to read easily.

4 Don't have too many columns in a chart or graph so that information has to be packed tightly together and can't be read easily.

5 Give diagrams, charts, graphs, etc., a title and, if necessary, give a brief outline of what they are about. Diagrams, graphs, charts, etc., should be self explanatory — it should be possible to understand them without having to look through a text.

6 Put the title and information above the diagram, chart, graph, etc.

7 Often non-textual information can be set out in more than one form, so a decision has to be made on which is most suitable in that instance. This is often a matter of personal choice, so try several different forms to see which one you think is best.

Look at the task sheets listed below in which information has been set out in a number of alternative ways to straight text.

What are the differences between the ways in which information is given?
Do you consider one form to be better than the other in each case? If so, why?
Could the information be given in another form which might make it clearer and easier to understand?

TASK SHEETS: 15, 15a

RESEARCH SKILLS

In order to become truly independent readers, students will need to develop their research skills. From the very beginning of the course, encourage students to find things for themselves. Make sure that they know the library system and where to find books, especially those that relate to their course. The library staff are always willing to give groups of students a short introduction to the library and explain how to find a book and use the other facilities in the library.

Text books are not usually read from cover to cover like a novel but are dipped into whenever a particular bit of information is required. Make sure that your students know how to find information in a text book, especially if there is a set text book which they are likely to use a lot.

Where possible, exercises that give practice in using research skills should be incorporated in normal course work since students find it easier to complete tasks that have a real purpose.

Choosing a Book

The process of finding the right book is a series of stages that starts with a casual glance at the cover and progresses to close reading of the text. Picking up any book and flicking through the pages may find the information that is needed, but it is very time-consuming. To save time in fruitless searching, most text books include a variety of aids to help people find the topic they are searching for. Make sure that students are aware of these aids and how to use them.

The first indication that a book may be suitable is, of course, the title. Publishers try to ensure that the title of a text book gives a concise description of what the book contains and possibly its intended reader, e.g. *GCSE Biology* or *Information Technology at Work*. But it is sometimes difficult to think of a new title that hasn't been used before. If the title is not clear, there is often, on the back, a brief summary of the objectives of the book and an indication of the level of study it is designed for.

If the book seems to be suitable, then you can begin to search for the information that you need. There are several ways in which this can be done and these are given later.

Other useful indicators of a book's suitability are:

- the name of the author – perhaps you have already read a book by the author and found it useful and interesting or it may be someone who is well known as an expert in that particular subject.

- the date of publication – the content and style of courses change over the years, and it is more likely that a recently published book will be relevant to current courses. There is a trend for text books to be written in a more accessible style and for information to be set out more clearly. Some older books have been revamped and are now much easier to use.

- a book from a series – some publishers have series of books on different study topics. They will have an editor who will ensure that there is a consistent style and approach throughout the series. It may be that when studying another subject you have used a book in the same series and found it useful.

T A S K

Look through the list of books and choose which ones you think would contain the information that you need.
Why did you choose some books and not others?

TASK SHEET: 16

Categories

Make sure that students can identify the topic/subject/general category under which they could find specific information.

This skill is mostly about how well students are able to classify things. For example, when engineering students are looking for information about aluminium, they should be aware that it may be included in a section about 'non-ferrous metals'. Or, in a more general engineering book it may be found in a section on 'metals' or even 'engineering materials'.

Teaching students to compile charts like the one below gives them good practice for developing their classification skills.

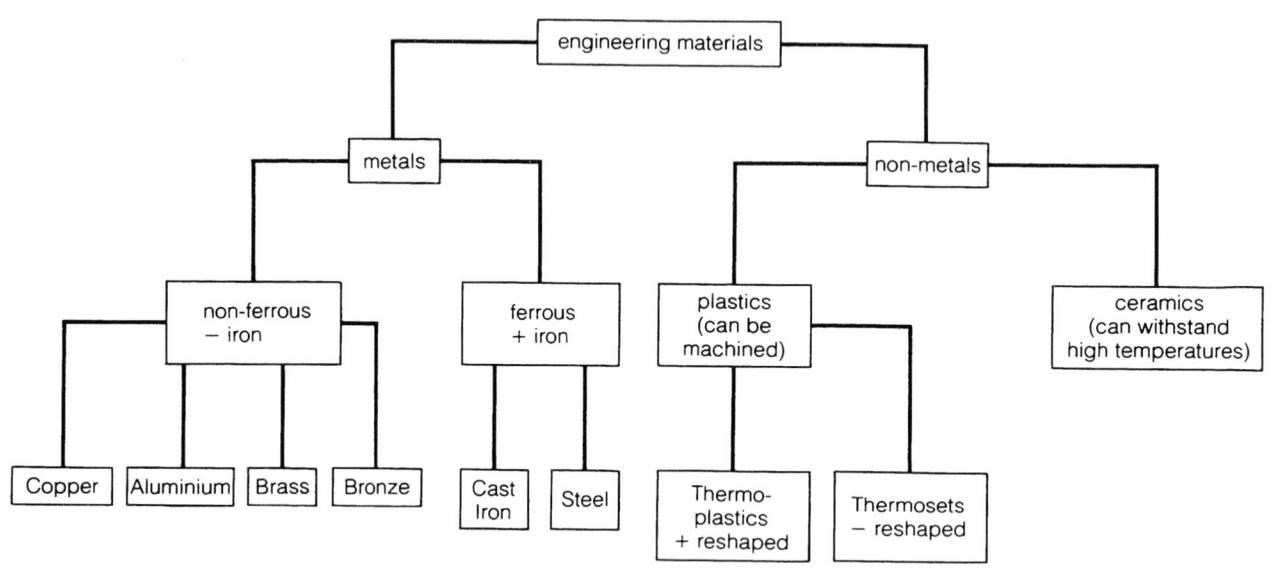

TASK

Things can be classified in a variety of ways. There are numerous criteria which can determine the particular sub-groups of any one main group. These criteria are mostly the properties that make things similar or different.

Look at the picture of methods of transport and try to decide the various criteria which could be applied to show similarities and differences between them. Make a column for each criterion and mark a plus sign against the method of transport where that criterion applies and a minus sign where it doesn't. If a criterion applies at some times but not always, mark a plus and minus sign. The first column 'It is powered by an engine' has been filled in as an example.

Eventually, you should have about eight criteria. Wherever there is a plus sign in a column, the method of transport could be classified in this way.

TASK SHEET: 17

Give students exercises in using the index and contents pages to find the page references for information that they need.

Early on in the course, set questions which practise using the index and contents of books that are likely to be used fairly often. Some books will have good indexes and contents, so page references can be found very easily. In other books it may be more difficult.

When students are working independently, indexes and contents will provide them with initial indicators as to whether the book they have selected will contain the information they require. However, they must be aware that the topic or item that they are searching for won't always be listed in its alphabetical order but may be included under a general category heading.

T A S K

> Look through the Contents and Index of one of your course books and try to find on which page of the book you would be able to read about a specific topic.
>
> Then try to analyse how you found the page number; what skills did you have to use? Obviously, if you knew a lot about that topic then it should not have been too hard. But what about someone who doesn't know; where do they start to look? Is there a key word which helps them? Do they have to use any categorisation skills?
>
> *TASK SHEETS: 18, 18a*

Headings and Sub-headings

Develop the students' ability to look through a book using the headings and sub-headings, if there are any, to select which part of a page they need to read.

Again this might require students to use classification skills. Being able to use headings and sub-headings is useful where books do not have a contents list or index.

9
Preservation of foods

Preservation

This may be achieved by several methods:

(a) By removing the moisture from the food, e.g. drying, dehydration.

(b) By making the food cold, e.g. chilling, freezing.

(c) By app

(d) By rad

(e) By che

Food may be

1 Drying
2 Dehydr
3 Chilling
4 Freezing

Chilling and freezing

Refrigeration is a method of preservation where the micro-organisms are not killed; they are only prevented from multiplying. The lower the temp temperat a short ti at −28°C required

Advantages of using frozen foods

(a) Frozen foods are ready-prepared, therefore there is a saving of time and labour.

(b) Portion control and costing are easily assessed.

(c) Foods are always 'in season'.

(d) Compact storage.

(e) Additional stocks to hand.

(f) Guaranteed quality.

For example, catering students might be asked to look through the chapter on 'Preserving Food' in *The Theory of Catering* and find the advantages of using frozen foods. They would not be able to find a page reference in either the contents or index so they will have to look through the chapter a page at a time. Fortunately there are headings and sub-headings so they need only glance at each of these to see whether the information they need is included in that section of the page. Eventually they will come to the sub-heading 'Advantages of using frozen food'.

T A S K

> Look through the list of headings and sub-headings and state under which of these you are likely to find the information that you require.
> Was there anything which helped you in your choice?
> - a particular word in your question?
> - a particular word in the heading?
> - information that you already had?
>
> *TASK SHEET: 19*

Skimming

Where a book does not have a comprehensive contents or index and the text is not broken up under headings and sub-headings, the students will have to skim through the book. This involves reading the first sentence of each paragraph to find which section they will have to read more fully for the information that they need. The first sentence will usually give a good indication of what that paragraph is about, so skimming through will avoid reading those parts that are not of immediate interest to the students.

T A S K

> Choose a short piece of text (about a page).
> Read through the first sentence in each paragraph of the text and write a brief note of what each paragraph is about.
>
> *TASK SHEET: 20*

Scanning

This is an alternative strategy to skimming. Here the students look through a text trying to find particular keywords. Whenever they find a keyword, they read the sentence to see if the information they require is there.

T A S K

> Do the exercise set out on task sheet 21 or devise one yourself using the example as a guide.
>
> *TASK SHEET: 21*

Give students practice at scanning by asking them to look through passages and underline keywords.

The following task is useful for making students aware of the overall structure of text; it also encourages close reading of a text. If students can see that there is some logical progression in a text, then they may be able to skip through parts to get to the particular section they require. If they only need some information on the latter stages of a process then they do not need to read the first part of the text. If they appreciate that there is a logical structure to texts and understand how this operates, they will be able to transfer this understanding to their own writing later.

T A S K

Look at the paragraphs from a text which have been jumbled up. Read through them and then try to rearrange them to their original order.

TASK SHEET: 22

CHALK
AND
TALK

INTRODUCTION

Spoken language is the largest ingredient of any classroom or workshop. It serves a variety of functions and exists in a variety of forms. At one extreme is a teacher delivering a formal lecture to a silent audience. At the other extreme is the chatter of a classroom where groups of students are involved in several different conversations. Both processes have a place in learning, and the balance between them will vary according to the objectives of the lesson.

For effective learning to take place, several points need to be borne in mind.

- Teachers should be constantly aware of the language that they use and whether this is appropriate to the level of the students to whom they are talking.
- Teachers should be aware of how they organise their talk and try to ensure that there is a logical development from one point to the next.
- Within that development, they must employ methods which allow the students to assimilate new concepts and vocabulary into their existing knowledge. It is no use talking to students about matters which they are not as yet familiar with, unless it is done in a way that they will readily understand.

TEACHING METHODS

There are several methods of learning which require spoken language and any lesson will contain a mixture of these. We examine some of them below together with the auxiliary aids available. First, there are a few general issues which need to be considered.

Current recommendations on classroom practice state that more emphasis should be placed on promoting student discussion. No one would deny that discussion should play a greater role in learning than it has generally done in the past: its advantages and benefits are well documented. Yet though discussion, in theory, ought to result in effective learning, it sometimes fails because of the attitude of the students. Some students expect the lesson to be teacher-dominated. They don't feel that they are learning unless they are having information handed out to them, and so they don't actively participate in discussion. Some students feel more secure in a formal lesson. They like the familiar structure and understand the implicit rules which govern how and when they are expected to talk. For them, discussion demands too much public participation. You need to prepare students like this carefully for the less formal lesson. Let them know the purpose of the lesson and what you hope will be its outcome.

Whatever method of learning you choose, there should always be clear objectives to be achieved by the end of a lesson. It is easy in discussion groups for students to wander from what is strictly relevant. Although in one respect, students should be encouraged to use their language to explore all possibilities, some unobtrusive guidance is likely to be necessary.

The arrangement of the classroom sometimes creates problems for certain methods of learning. Too much time can be taken up trying to organise small discussion groups in a classroom set out for a more formal lesson. In a small classroom, the proximity of groups can be a distraction, so that students do not concentrate solely on what is being said in their group. Auxiliary aids may not be easily visible to the whole group because of the brightness or layout of the room. There may not be enough electric sockets in a room or they may be placed in inconvenient places. Unless arrangements can be made for an alternative room, you may have to think of a way to minimise the problem. All these physical aspects have to be taken into consideration when deciding what methods of learning are going to be used.

When planning lessons, remember that there are a variety of approaches which can be used. Some obviously lend themselves to certain topics rather than others and some students will learn more from one form of lesson rather than another. Varying the methods of learning keeps students interested and ensures that their different abilities can be accommodated.

Advantages and Disadvantages of Different Teaching Methods

■ Lecture

Advantages
1 Can be used to present specialised or current information not widely available.
2 Some people find it easier to learn from the spoken rather than the written word.
3 Useful for introducing, recapitulating or revising a topic.
4 Teacher has control of lesson format.

Disadvantages
1 Only one-way communication.
2 Autocratic – prevents free exchange of ideas.
3 No feedback on what learning is taking place.
4 Pre-defined – doesn't allow for a change of approach.

Points to consider
Can the students read the information elsewhere?
Provide the students with an active listening exercise.
Try to use a visual aid to focus the students' attention.
Provide natural breaks for alternative activities.

■ Demonstration

Advantages
1 Easier to learn from a visual presentation.
2 Can be used to inform of specialised skills.
3 Useful for learning skills, understanding theories and concepts, visualising processes.
4 Teacher has control of lesson format.

Disadvantages

1 Only one-way communication.
2 Autocratic – prevents free exchange of ideas.
3 No feedback on what learning is taking place.
4 Pre-defined – doesn't allow for a change of approach.
5 Difficult to retain all information.
6 Not conducive to note-taking.

Points to consider
Can learning be done through practical activities such as discovery learning or following an instruction sheet?
Provide natural breaks for alternative activities.
Set aside time for making notes.

■ **Questioning**

Advantages

1 Immediate feedback that some learning is taking place.
2 Students will be more attentive if they think they might be asked a question.
3 Can help to focus attention on keypoints.
4 Student participation.

Disadvantages

1 Teacher has less control of lesson format.
2 Participation of only a few.
3 Can lead to closed discussion – students trying to guess what the teachers want and usually restricted to one word answers.

Points to consider
Try to ensure that the questions require an open answer, not just the 'correct' answer.
Set questions which could lead to small group discussions.
Use students' answers to make notes or summarise points.

■ **Whole class discussion**

Advantages

1 Student-centred – students learn from their own and each others' experience and knowledge.
2 Immediate feedback that some learning is taking place.
3 Useful follow-up to lecture, for recapitulation and revision.
4 Helps to clarify information.
5 Exploration of ideas.

Disadvantages

1 Teacher has less control of lesson format.
2 Requires knowledge of topic.
3 Participation of a few.
4 Needs changes of classroom arrangement.

Points to consider
Preparation of topic by students through prior reading.
Preparation of guiding questions by teacher.
Try to encourage participation by all.
Try to keep effective control by establishing a few rules.
Be a good listener.
Write summaries of discussion on board – either teacher or student.

■ Small group discussion

Advantages
1 Student-centred – students learn from their own and each others' experience and knowledge.
2 Helps clarify information.
3 Exploration of ideas.
4 Participation of many.

Disadvantages
1 Teacher has little control of learning process.
2 Requires knowledge of topic.
3 May need changes of classroom arrangement.
4 Noise level.

Points to consider
Provide guidance on objectives – concrete outcomes such as charts on similarities/differences or advantages/disadvantages – public presentation such as short talk or poster.
Provide guidance on discussion format and language used by visiting each group periodically.

■ Practical

Advantages
1 Experiential learning.
2 Exploration of ideas.
3 Participation of many.
4 Hands-on experience.

Disadvantages
1 Teacher has less control of learning.
2 Teacher has less control of lesson format.

Points to consider
Make sure the students have clear instruction of the task.
Stipulate what the outcome should be, e.g. 'What did you observe?'/ 'What did you achieve?'
Prepare safety aspect through prior discussion or safety film.

■ Role play

Advantages
1 Experiential learning.
2 Exploration of ideas.

Disadvantages
1 Teacher has less control of learning.
2 Teacher has less control of lesson format.
3 Reticence of some students.
4 Noise level.
5 May need changes of classroom arrangement.

Points to consider
Give the students clearly defined roles and objectives.
Set a time limit.
Have some form of group evaluation, perhaps through the use of video.

Audio-visual aids provide valuable illustrative material and are a useful device for focusing the students' attention. They also provide good aids to memory, since the students are receiving information through several of their senses. Audio-visual aids can, however, create problems over note-taking. During a demonstration, for example, if students attempt to write something down, they may well end up missing vital information. It is better to set aside a time for writing and to make sure that students are informed of this beforehand. Remember that you can use most audio-visual aids again, so take time to prepare good materials and store them carefully. Audio-visual aids should be an integral part of a lesson and not used merely as a teacher substitute.

Some audio-visual aids can be used for individuals or small group learning. Most students are now familiar with the operation of cassettes and videos; being able to pause at certain points or to replay material caters well for the different abilities in a classroom.

ADVANTAGES AND DISADVANTAGES OF SOME AUDIO-VISUAL AIDS

EQUIPMENT	ADVANTAGES	DISADVANTAGES
Chalkboard/ whiteboard	Cheap Plentiful and accessible Useful for focusing on and emphasising key points to be built on and referred back to during lesson Flexible – can respond to needs as they occur Can provide natural break in lesson	Material not re-usable Time-consuming during lesson Can interrupt flow of lesson Static (though some boards can be moved within classroom)
Magnetic board	Can prepare complicated maps/diagrams/charts, etc., prior to lesson Materials are re-usable	Requires special materials which are not always available Not all classrooms have magnetic boards
Flip charts	Can prepare complicated material prior to lesson Re-usable Portable Useful for sequential presentations	Cannot easily be referred back to Small – limits amount of information that can be presented at one time
Models	Three-dimensional Useful for illustrating detail and complex processes Re-usable	Time-consuming to make
Radio broadcast/ audio tape	Introduction of expert into the classroom Tapes can be used by small groups or individuals and can be replayed	Less control of duration Less control of language used Needs a focusing device if used with large group
Film/TV/video	Introduction of expert into the classroom Introduction of 'reality' into the classroom Expands presentation beyond confines of classroom Videos can be used by small groups or individuals and can be replayed	Less control of duration Less control of language used

EQUIPMENT	ADVANTAGES	DISADVANTAGES
OHP	Can be used like a chalkboard Can prepare materials beforehand Some commercial materials available Can use photocopied materials (with correct acetate in photocopier) Information can be gradually revealed in sequence Maps/charts/diagrams, etc., can be gradually built up using overlays	Not always clearly visible in a bright room
Slides	Introduction of 'reality' into classroom Expands presentation beyond confines of classroom Can be used in conjunction with an audio tape Possible to produce own slides without too much effort or expense	Requires special equipment which is not always available Needs a darkened room – not always available Commentary might have to be made from the back of the class – can make it less audible
Illustrations/ texts	Provides focus during talk Provides students with permanent reference material Can be used for small group and individual work	Might be at inappropriate level for ability of students
Computers	Useful for simulation exercises Small group of individual work	Not available in all rooms
Visits/work	Students learn through all their senses: sight, sound, touch, smell, maybe even taste Provides excellent source materials for further activities	Not easily controlled by teacher Time-consuming in planning and execution

Delivery

Ability to hear

Because it is the most obvious consideration, it is one that is often overlooked. Make sure that all students can hear you.

Knowledge of the language

Some students will have a restricted range of vocabulary and will possibly not be familiar with certain phrases (e.g. in order to, is likely to) or idioms and colloquial terms (e.g. down in the mouth, turn over a new leaf).

To help students understand, there are several strategies which you can use:

1 **Speed**
   Students need time to think about what is being said, especially as most of this will be new information and vocabulary they are not familiar with. You can give them time by refraining from speaking too quickly and, if necessary, pausing after giving important pieces of information.

2 **Planned repetition**
   Repeating important pieces of information will also give the students time to think about what is being said and maybe translate it into language that they can easily understand. There are several ways that this can be done.
   a) Repetition – saying the same thing again.   [*continued on page 41*]

1 Make sure that the board is clean at the beginning of each lesson.

2 Write neatly and legibly so that students at the back of the room can easily read what you write.

3 Use lower case letters (i.e. NOT CAPITALS) as these can be read much more easily and quickly.

4 Use colour to differentiate and highlight different types of information.

5 Present information as it occurs rather than all at once. This helps students follow the structure of what they are being told and prevents them being distracted by information that is not immediately relevant.

6 Don't crowd the board or OHP – too much information crammed closely together can be confusing and off-putting.

7 Don't write things down haphazardly – an ordered sequence is easier to follow.

8 When writing down a word to show students how it is spelt:
- explain the meaning before writing the word, as this gives more impact
- write it as it occurs
- say the word as you write it
- encourage the students to use it by asking questions
- ask the students to write it down

These points also apply for introducing new structures, idioms, colloquial terms and abbreviations.

9 Check your spelling from time to time by standing back from the board.

10 Don't use abbreviations unless you are sure that the students know what they mean.

11 If students have to copy information from the board or OHP, leave space for them to fill in keywords. This makes them think about what they are writing and is good spelling practice.

12 But include a list of the missing words at the bottom of the board or OHP. If students have to guess the spelling, this can reinforce spelling errors.

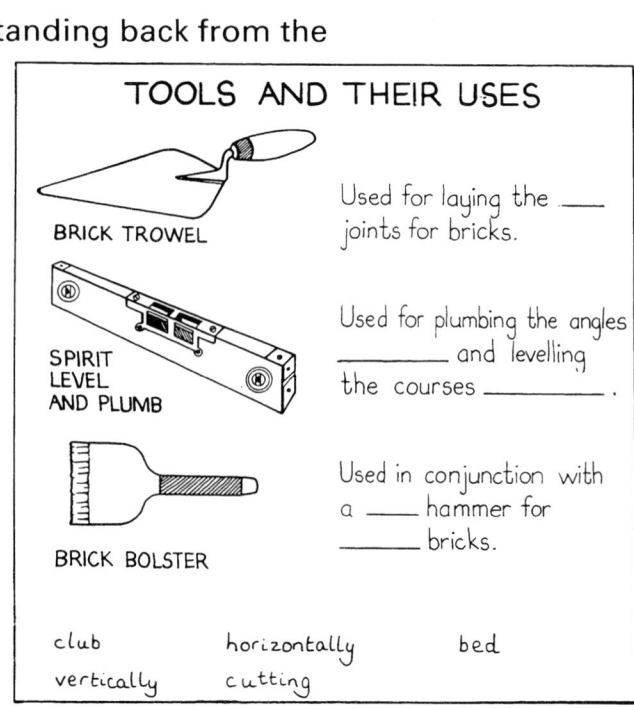

TOOLS AND THEIR USES

BRICK TROWEL — Used for laying the ___ joints for bricks.

SPIRIT LEVEL AND PLUMB — Used for plumbing the angles _____ and levelling the courses _____.

BRICK BOLSTER — Used in conjunction with a ___ hammer for _____ bricks.

club   horizontally   bed

vertically   cutting

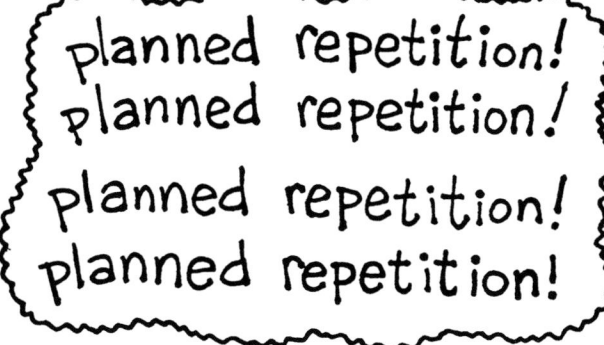

b) Re-formulation – saying the same thing but in a different way.

    e.g.   Cover the dish in order to prevent air being admitted.
           Cover the dish to stop air getting in.
           A rule of thumb is to halve the result and add six.
           A way of guessing what the answer will be is to halve the result and add six.

c) Summary – briefly going over points that have been mentioned earlier.

3 Segmented information

Too much information at one time is difficult to take in. Most students will not be able to concentrate for more than fifteen minutes at a time and will quickly become bored if they have to listen for longer. Try to give information in a maximum of fifteen minute chunks interspersed with different activities e.g. small group discussion, writing tasks, practical work.

Initially, these different activities need only last for five minutes but the longer the lesson lasts, the longer the activities should be allowed to run for.

Segmented information gives the students time to think about what has been said and keeps them more alert and attentive for new information.

Spelling

If you introduce a word which the students are likely to use and might find difficult to spell, write it on the board or OHP. Only do this as the word occurs. You may need to do it on several occasions to make sure the students can spell the word. Other useful strategies are listed in the section on the use of the board and OHP.

Dictation

Dictation is often a fruitless exercise. Some students won't be able to write notes from dictation and so will not retain the information that they need. There are many reasons for this:

■ Hearing difficulty
■ Restricted knowledge of the language
    If students hear a word they don't know, they may try to guess and put down the wrong word. Because they are concentrating on writing down individual words, they are not concerned about whether it fits in with the meaning of the sentence.

■ Spelling difficulties
  If students are having to think about how to spell a word, they may miss out the words that immediately follow it. If they have to guess the spelling, they may not understand what it is supposed to be when they re-read their notes.
■ Slow writers
  If students cannot keep up with the speed of dictation, they will miss out chunks of information.

What to do instead of dictation

Give out copies of the notes or passage that you intended to dictate, but leave some key words out. The students will then have to fill these in themselves. But give the copies out before the session so the students know what to listen for.

The Active Listening exercises mentioned next are another way or avoiding dictation.

ENCOURAGING AND DEVELOPING LISTENING SKILLS

Don't allow students to be passive listeners during a lesson. There is no immediate way of assessing what passive listeners have learnt. Some teachers may use a question and answer technique but this only indicates what has been learnt by those who care to respond. Also, as passive listeners, the students have no record of what they are expected to learn. Handouts or notes can be given out at the end of the lesson but usually these are immediately put in a book or folder so that when they are brought out later, the students don't fully understand what they are about.

During a lesson, therefore, encourage students to become active listeners. Make them listen for key information and write it down. Doing this successfully indicates that they have understood what information they have been given. Being active listeners will make them more alert and attentive. But, more importantly, being active listeners gives the students useful practice in using the language that they need for the subject that they are studying.

Active Listening

There are several ways to encourage students to be active listeners and develop their listening skills. These are similar to those already illustrated in the section on Reading. Like the reading skills exercises, active listening exercises also prepare students for written work, since they develop the ability to express themselves clearly, concisely and comprehensively.

As previously stated, students should initially be given simple exercises which require little input from them; gradually the amount of input from the students should be increased.

The types of exercises students can be given are:
- gapped handouts
- multiple choice questions
- true/false statements
- completing lists
- completing charts
- labelling diagrams

_T A S K_

Look at each of the worksheets and try to complete them from what you know already or try to guess what the missing information might be. Then listen once to the section of the script (or get someone to read it out if you have not recorded it) which relates to each of the worksheets and fill in any missing information or check that what you have already written is correct.

SCRIPTS: 1–6   *TASK SHEETS: 23–28*

When devising active listening exercises, try to ensure that they are testing the students' understanding and that they are identifying key points of information. Remember to give the exercise out before beginning the lecture or demonstration and allow a few minutes for students to look through the exercise. Encourage them to fill in any parts they know already or make considered guesses on what the missing information might be. Unlike the active reading exercise, students are only going to hear information once. They cannot keep referring back to look for any information they might have missed. It is better, therefore, to present the exercise in the same chronological order as it is likely to occur in the lecture or demonstration.

As an initial preparation, some active listening exercises could be done using a cassette tape. Students can then listen more than once if they fail to pick out the correct information. It provides an opportunity to identify any particular difficulties students may have and to focus on these. Small sections can then be replayed and discussed.

Tapes can also be used for students to work individually or in small groups so that the different abilities within a classroom can be accommodated.

TASK

The titles of the talks and discussions for developing listening skills are:
- The floppy disk
- The principle of scanning
- If you smell gas . . .
- Types of motor vehicle
- The reasons for the changes in agriculture

- The advantages and dis-advantages of felt
- Cheques
- The role of local councils in leisure and recreation
- A day in the life . . .

Try to determine the language function of each of these (e.g. narrative, instruction, description, etc.).

Using the appropriate list of questions you have drawn up for the Keypoint Questions, see how many of the questions you can answer from what you know about the subject. Then listen to the tape and fill in as much information as you can from what is said on the tape or check that the information that you have already filled in is correct.

If you have not drawn up a list of questions for a keypoint checklist, refer back to pages 22–24 of the Reading section to see how to do this.

SCRIPTS: 1–9

Because you are unable to survey a text when thinking about the information that is likely to be given in a talk or discussion, it is much harder to predict what questions might be answered. This is particularly difficult when the title of the talk or discussion is ambiguous. For example, in the case of the floppy disk text, you do not know whether you are going to be told how to do something, whether you are going to be given a description or whether the advantages and disadvantages are going to be given.

It is important, therefore, when you begin a talk or discussion that you make it clear what sort of information the students should be listening for.

SMALL GROUP WORK

Students should not always be listeners. Opportunities for them to be speakers have to be created. It is an important part of education. Students must have a chance to talk about their learning so that they formulate and reformulate their knowledge as they encounter new ideas and information. It is helpful to 'talk things through' with someone even if they only give looks of approval or disapproval. Students also have to have an opportunity to develop their oral skills so that they will feel confident about expressing themselves to the world beyond the classroom. An essential part of education is to prepare students to be effective citizens.

It has already been stated that the question/answer process has only a limited use in the classroom. Usually only a few students choose to respond. The sort of responses that are made are often restricted by the form of questioning employed, and the public nature of the activity can lead to expression of accepted prejudices rather than explorations of personal opinions.

Most of these problems are overcome through involving students in small group work. This can take the form of a practical activity, a discussion or role play, and the advantages, disadvantages and points of good practice for each have been set out earlier. Whatever subject a student is studying, there will be new vocabulary and different forms of expression to learn, technical terms and new concepts to be mastered. Through small group work, students are able to assimilate this new knowledge in terms which they more readily understand. This assimilation occurs at the students' own pace. It encourages co-operation and exchanges of ideas between students of differing abilities. Because students are talking with their peers, they can air new ideas in a less threatening environment without fear of ridicule.

As well as the benefits outlined above, discussion helps students use and extend their academic skills which they may subsequently transfer to their written work, such as reports or essays. There are many skills which the students should be encouraged to use:

- *analysis* – listening and thinking carefully about what is being said

- *comparing and contrasting* – showing how things are similar or different

- *criticising* – pointing out any flaws in a statement or making counter-claims

- *supporting* – extending ideas expressed by others, reformulating ideas and offering further evidence

- *persuading* – offering alternative ideas and trying to convince others through carefully structured argument

- *avoiding prejudgement* – listening to statements without bias or allowing others to put their point of view

- *fact and opinion* – being able to distinguish between what someone thinks and what can be shown to be true

- *generalising and exemplifying* – being able to offer particular examples to illustrate a general statement

Doing practical work in small groups also has the benefits outlined above including the promotion of discussion. Practical work also helps students use and extend their social skills:

- requesting

- offering

- suggesting

- refusing

- explaining

- negotiating

Most of the tasks in the section on Reading could provide useful stimuli for small group activities. Illustrations of other types of activities are also given at the back of the book. These cover such things as:

- case studies

- comparing and contrasting

- pointing out advantages and disadvantages

- exemplifying

Involving your students in small group work allows you to observe them and see how language is being used and how appropriately. You can then advise and help students on their use of language on a more individual and informal basis.

T A S K

Working in small groups, complete the task.

TASK SHEETS: 29, 30, 31

WRITING

INTRODUCTION

Several examples of how to develop students' writing skills have already been given in the previous sections of this book. These have been concerned with showing students which information is included in particular types of writing and how the presentation of this information is structured. This includes not only the extracts from textbooks, newspapers and magazines, but also some of the active reading and listening exercises which provide models for making notes. It is important that students are given good models of the different forms and styles of writing and that they are aware of the features that make them good models.

Writing is the most demanding of the language skills. This is not only because writing requires more physical effort than talking, listening and reading, or that writing takes more time, but also because it requires more precision.

In order to achieve that precision, several preparatory stages need to be gone through. Firstly, we need to clarify our thoughts so that when we put pen to paper, we are certain about what we want to say. Secondly, we need to organise our thoughts so that there is a lucid progression from one point to the next. Thirdly, we need to select the words we want to use so that we can write concisely and accurately. And finally, we need to ensure that what we write complies with the conventions of writing, such as appropriate style, grammar, spelling and punctuation. Obviously, we do not develop writing skills through a gradual progression from one stage to the next, and there will be several processes occurring at the same time.

But writing, of course, is not the final stage of the process alone; we use writing at every stage. We use it to record information, or as an aid to memory as we listen, read, evaluate and eventually formulate our thoughts and ideas. Like an artist preparing to paint a picture, we need to make sketches of all the ingredients and how these are going to be arranged before we create our final masterpiece.

We mentioned earlier that dictation should be avoided for several reasons. One further reason is that, in taking dictation, students miss out on these valuable preparatory stages. Similarly, students should be discouraged from copying materials from textbooks and handouts. Writing should be an indication of what the students themselves have learned and understood, not the ideas and thoughts of someone else.

The previous two sections on Reading and Chalk and Talk have included initial elements of the writing process. The active reading and listening exercises and the keypoint checklists are all ways of clarifying what the main points are which need to be included in any subsequent writing. This section will now take the process further and show how these initial writings can be organised into notes. These notes can then be referred to directly for classwork for an extended piece of writing such as an essay, report or project. Alternatively, they may be kept for later reference and committed to memory as an aid to answering examination questions. This section also shows how to take these notes, or a similar structure, and develop them into an extended piece of writing. There is also a section on basic skills which suggests strategies that can be used to help students who have problems with spelling and punctuation. And finally there is a short section on how to prepare students for tests and examinations.

NOTE MAKING

The way in which people make notes is very much a personal matter. Some people just write down the information they need, others prefer to set it out in a more graphic form. Some examples of ways in which notes can be set out are given on task sheets 32, 32a and 32b, but it is really up to individuals to sort out the form which suits them best. However, you can still recommend forms which are most suited for recording particular types of information and give the students good models of note-taking. Whatever form they choose, there are several things which should always be borne in mind.

Appropriate Types of Notes

The chart below shows which sorts of notes can be used for various types of writing. Sometimes the information being recorded will lend itself to one form of notes rather than another. At first students will probably have to be guided on how notes are to be set out but it would be useful to discuss what form of notes they find most helpful. Eventually they will have to set out their notes, so the students should be aware of why one form is chosen rather than another for a particular piece of writing.

	Linear	Flow Chart	Tabular Chart	Tree Diagram	Spider-gram	Diagram
Narrative Biography: report description of event	√	√	√	–	√	√ + map
Description Structure	√	–	√	–	√	√
Description Process	√	√	√	–	√	√ + map
Instruction	√	√	√	–	–	√
Classification Compare/Contrast	√	–	√	√	√	√ + graph
Exemplifying General Principle/Rule	√	–	√	√	√	–
Cause/Effect	√	√	√	–	–	√
Advantage/ Disadvantage	√	–	√	–	–	–
Theme	√	√	√	√	√	√

NOTE MAKING CHECKLIST

1 Only use one side of the paper. This may seem like a wasteful use of paper, but writing on the reverse side often shows through and makes the notes difficult to read.

2 Make sure the writing is legible and tidy.

3 Don't cram everything together. Leave plenty of space between pieces of information. This not only makes them easier to read, but allows things to be added later if necessary.

4 Try to look for a structure to the information that can be used for setting out the notes.

5 Where appropriate, use numbered and lettered headings and sub-headings. It is easier to remember a list of things if they are numbered and lettered.

6 Use indentations under headings and sub-headings.

7 Use colour to underline headings and keywords.

8 Use circles or boxes to emphasise things or group them together.

9 Where possible, draw diagrams, maps or pictures.

    Language Guidelines © 1990 ALBSU. Published by Hodder & Stoughton.

TASK

Read through one of the sample texts and make rough notes on the essential information it contains.

TASK SHEETS: 9–12

Using the illustrations set out on the task sheets as a guide, see how many different ways you can write out your notes.

TASK SHEETS: 32, 32a, 32b

Look at the task sheets which show how notes can be set out in different ways.

TASK SHEETS: 33, 33a

When you have finished, decide which form of your notes you find the easiest to read or remember.

SQ3R

A successful strategy that has been used by many students as an over-all guide to study is a method known as SQ3R. The initials stand for:

Survey : Question : Read : Recall : Revise

The method fits in well with many of the strategies for developing the language skills of students which have been set out in this book.

Survey

- Pick out a book that looks as though it might contain the information that is required.
- Look through the contents and index pages.
- Look through the headings and sub-headings, if there are any.
- Skim through the initial sentences of chapters and paragraphs.
- Look at any summaries if there are any at the end of each chapter.
- Having found a passage or chapter that might be worth reading in more detail, try to determine what type of text it is (narrative, description, compare/contrast, etc.)
- If you are listening to a talk, try to predict what type of talk it will be.

Question

- Draw up a list of questions that you want answered.
- You may already have a list but, if not, use the keypoint questions (see page 126) to indicate what information you might expect.

Read

- Read the text closely.
- Listen closely.
- Try to answer all the questions on your list.
- Does the text or talk raise any further questions that are not on your list? If so, write them down.

Recall

- Have all your questions been answered?
- Read the text again to make sure.
- If you have been listening to a talk, try to remember what has been said.
- If you have any unanswered questions, can you find the information elsewhere? e.g. another book, elsewhere in the same book.
- If you have been listening to a talk, ask the speaker.

Revise

- Read through the answers to your questions and try to translate them into an appropriate note form.
- Check your notes to make sure that you understand them and that you have not left anything out.

Abbreviations

Notes are used mainly as a personal memory aid so it is not necessary to write all the information out in full. There are many ways in which words can be abbreviated or replaced by symbols so that they are easier to jot down. It can also be easier to read notes at a glance and memorise them if they are set out in an abbreviated form. Some abbreviations even become accepted for the more formal types of writing such as essays, reports and projects (VDU; carb; i.e.; TV). Make sure that students know the meaning of the abbreviations and symbols that they come across. Encourage them to make up their own abbreviations and symbols when they are making notes, but they must make sure that they will be able to understand them when they come to re-read their notes.

- Some common abbreviations:

g	grammes	e.g.	for example
m	metres	pt	part (point)
l	litres	diff	differs (different/
min	minutes		differential)
sec	seconds	N.B.	note well
cont	continued	shd	should
		cd	could

- Some common symbols:

$\therefore$	therefore	$=$	equals
$\because$	because	$\neq$	does not equal (is different
Fe	Iron		from)
H_2O	Water	$\rightarrow$	leads to (caused, until)
Na	Sodium	$\leftarrow$	is caused by (depends on)
		$+$	and (positive)

- Some abbreviations used in specific subjects:

SLR	Single Lens Reflex	CNS	Central Nervous System
DPC	Damp Proof Course	WW2	World War Two
T&G	Tongue and Groove	tdc	Top dead centre

Look at the list of words and decide how you might abbreviate them but still be able to understand what word they represent. Look at the list of abbreviations and decide what word they represent. There may be more than one answer.
Make up some abbreviations of your own and then pass them to a friend or colleague. Can he or she guess what your original word was?

TASK SHEET: 34

EXTENDED WRITING

When students are asked to do a piece of extended writing such as an essay or report, they often feel that they do not have to set pen to paper until they produce the finished piece of work. This usually leads to constant frustration when they realise that they have omitted an important piece of information or have mis-spelt words and have to start again. What many students do not appreciate is that time spent in thought and preparation can avoid this frustration and result in a better piece of writing.

When asking students to produce an extended piece of writing, it is useful to guide them through each of the preparatory stages, either by discussion or by getting them to submit rough drafts for approval before allowing them to proceed to the next stage.

Title

Many problems arise because the students do not read the title or instructions thoroughly or misunderstand exactly what they are being asked to do. Sometimes this occurs because they do not fully understand the instruction words such as 'define', 'evaluate' and 'summarise'. Or they may omit to read qualifying words such as 'briefly', 'the main' and 'recent'. They then waste time writing out more than they have to.

Time spent by the students in reading a title or instructions and thinking about exactly what it asks them to do (or not to do) is time well spent. So when giving the students a title or instruction, go through it with them, making sure that they understand what is expected from them.

The sort of question students could be asked might read:
Write *brief notes* on *four* of the *main* documents used in *trading*, making sure that in each case you indicate whom the document is *to and from*.
The important points are in italics.

■ *brief notes* – not too detailed; not necessarily in complete sentences.
■ *four* – not three or five.
■ *main* – the most important, e.g. order, invoice, delivery note, statement of account.
■ *trading* – between buyers and sellers, not banks, insurers, etc.
■ *to and from* – indicate who is the sender and who is the receiver for each.

Research

This topic has been dealt with previously in the 'Reading' section and advice and exercises on how to guide and develop students' research and reading skills are given there (see page 21). But here are a few points on how these skills can be applied.

Get the students to draw up a list of questions similar to those in the Keypoint Checklist (page 126) on the information they feel should be included in their piece of writing. This list could be discussed or submitted for approval, but students shouldn't be allowed to think that this is a definitive list. As they do their research, they should keep adding questions to the list until they feel that they have all the information that they need to answer fully the title or instruction they have been given. Initially, it will help students if they are given a few questions to get them started. It will also help if they are given the names of books, magazines, etc., where they can find the information they need. Also, stress that at this stage neatness is not essential and providing that the students themselves can read and understand what they have written, then that is adequate. It does not matter if words are crossed out or mis-spelt or if writing is crammed together and set out untidily.

Structure

Having collected the information, the students now need to decide how it is to be set out in their piece of writing. To do this, they should try to see if there is a logical structure. If the piece of writing is one of the types set out in the chart on note-taking (instruction, narrative, description, etc.) then this should not be too difficult. Indeed, if the students are able to transfer their information into the appropriate note form, this will suggest how their writing should be structured and will make it easier to ensure that all the information is included in the final piece. Whether this is possible or not, a rough plan of how the information is to be set out should be drawn up. Examples of how this can be done are given on the next few pages with the final ordering of information numbered. Get the students to make similar plans briefly stating each point but again stress that neatness is not important.

Narrative (including description of event, description of process, instruction, and biography)

In note form, narrative stages are all usually written chronologically in linear notes or a flow chart (see on the next page) and the same chronological sequence is suitable for extended pieces of writing. The introduction will probably include an overall description followed by a brief explanation of the number and names of the various stages. Each stage will include elements such as how, when, where and why something happened. The conclusion could include such things as the eventual outcome or a personal comment by the student on any benefits or disadvantages that have resulted.

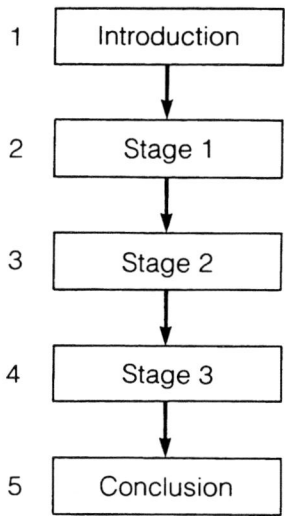

Description of a structure

When describing an object, students should look for a logical way to do this. Depending on the make-up of the object it can be done in one of several ways. They could begin by describing the outside or an outer layer and then each subsequent layer until they reach the middle. Or they could start on the left hand side of the object and work across to the right, or the top of the object and work to the bottom. Or they could describe each part as it occurs in a clockwise direction.

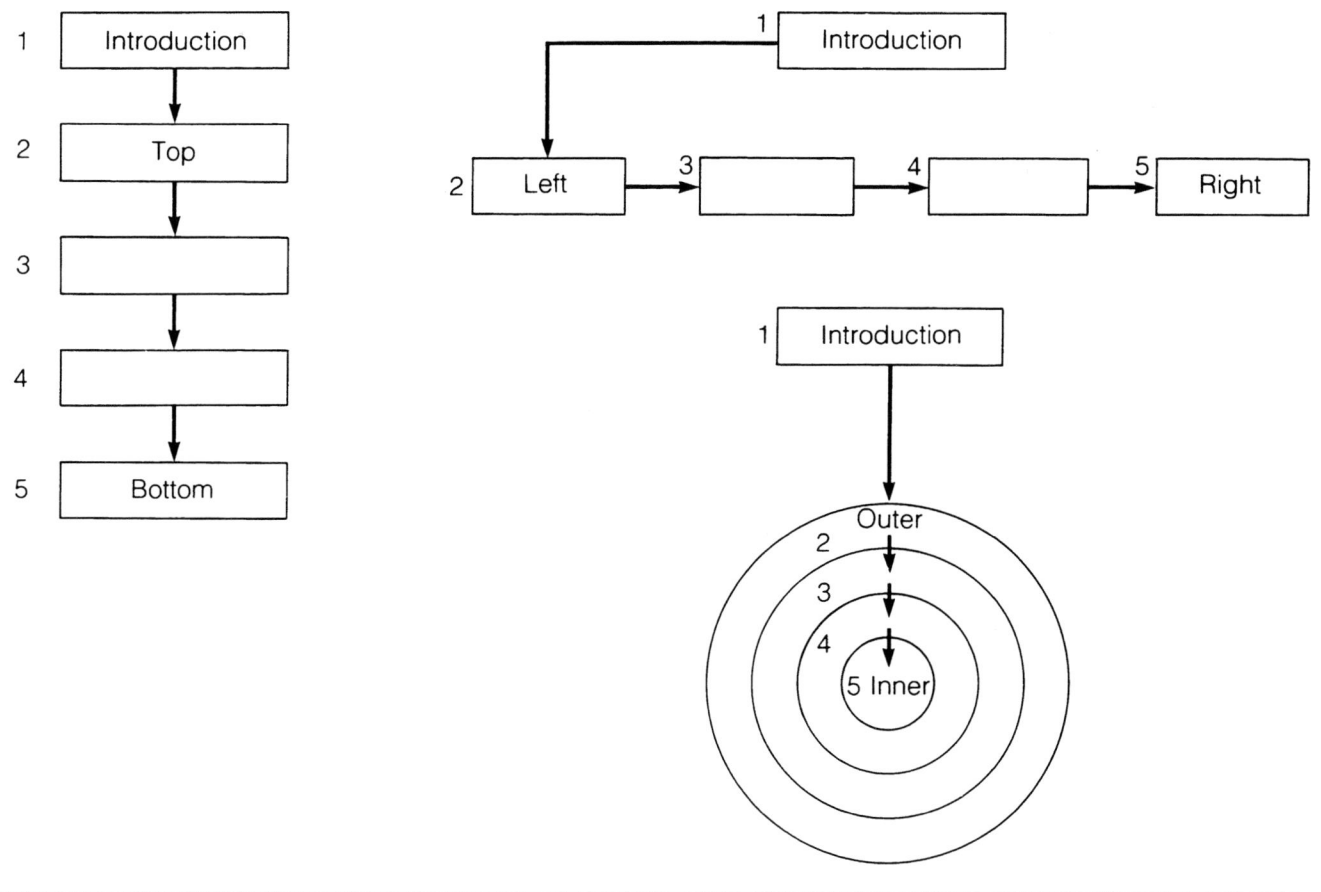

Classification

Like its preferred note form, classification is best set out in a tree diagram or spidergram. The final ordering of information is taken by following each of the branches to its termination working from left to right. The various sub-categories, into which each main category is divided, should be clearly named or labelled before any of these are detailed.

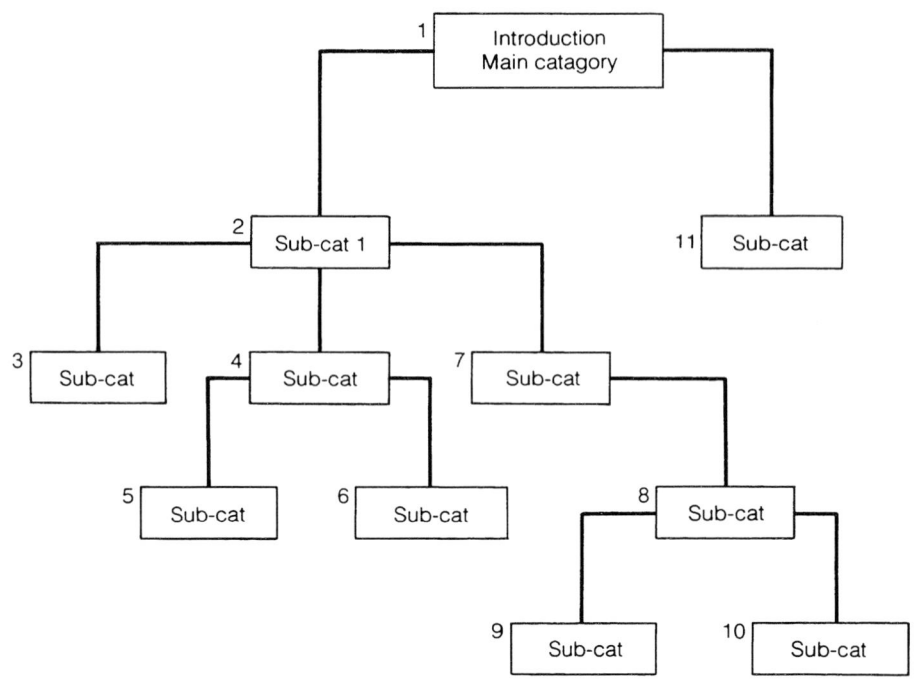

Cause/Effect

After stating the main cause, the effects that this has or had can be set out. Or conversely, after stating the main effect, the various things which cause or caused it can be set out. It may be that an effect, in turn, becomes the cause of something else, e.g. CFC gases reduce the ozone layer; reduction of the ozone layer increases penetration of ultra violet rays; ultra violet rays cause skin cancer. Or a cause may have an effect in addition to the one mentioned initially. The conclusion could include a brief summary of the various interactions or a comment on what these interactions are leading to.

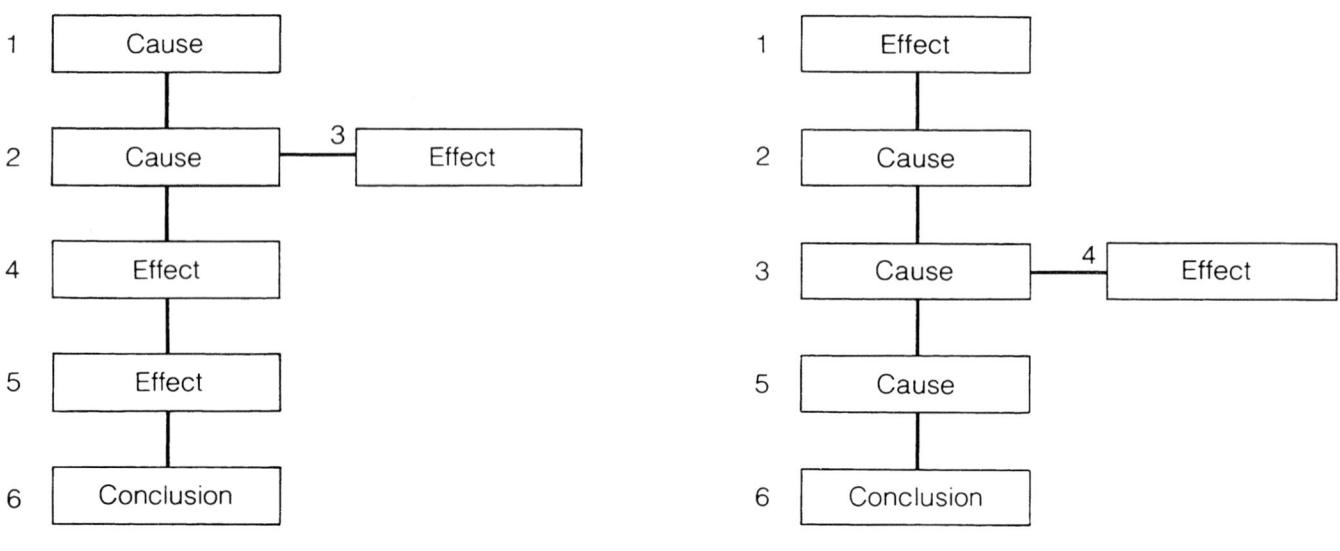

**Advantage/
Disadvantage**

For a short piece of writing it is better to name all the advantages first and then the disadvantages. For a longer piece, it is better to counterbalance the various advantages and disadvantages alternately. The conclusion will usually express a personal view of whether the advantages outweigh the disadvantages or vice-versa.

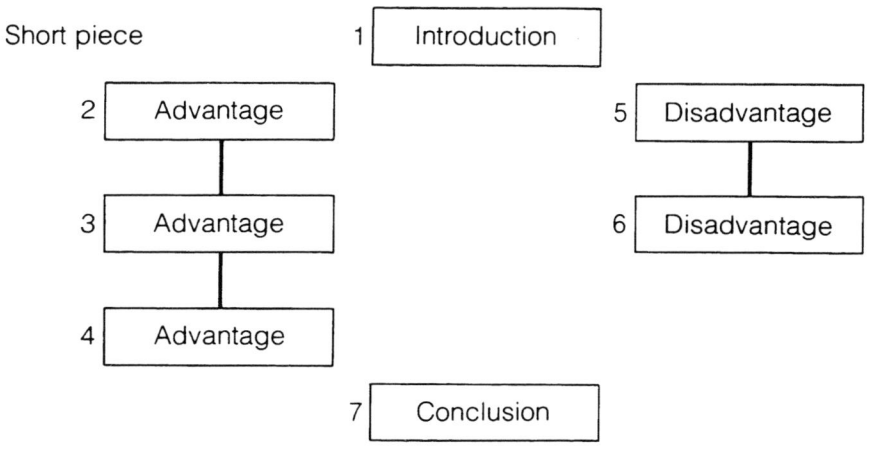

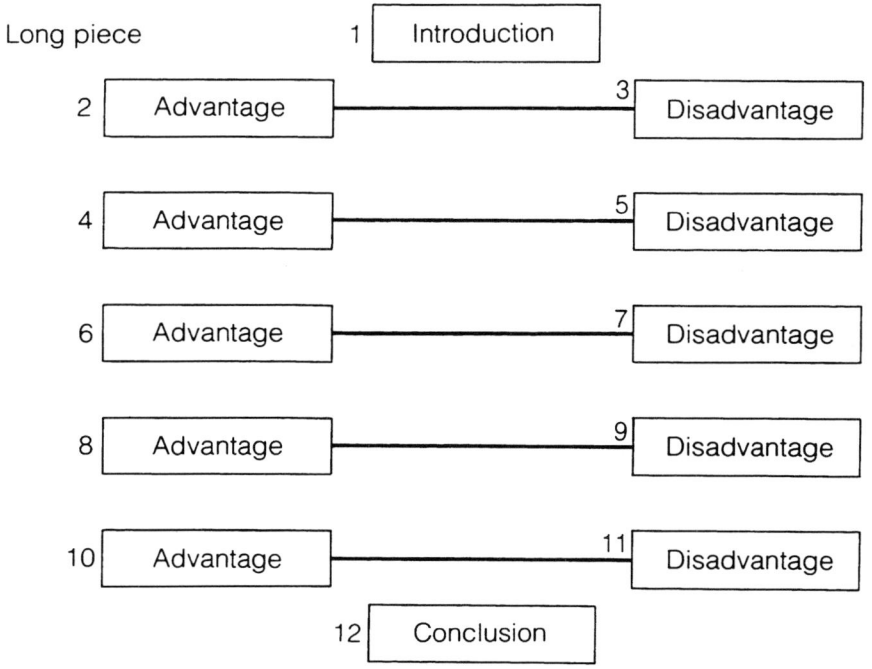

TASK

Look at some different types of sample texts and try to determine if there is a logical structure to the way they have been set out.
Does this structure match any of those given as examples in this book?
If not, why not? Is there a particular reason for the text to be set out in the way that it has?

TASK SHEETS: 4–12

Style

1 Once you have collected all the information you need and decided on the appropriate structure for the piece of writing, you should decide on the style of your writing and how formal or informal it should be.
This will depend on:
a) who is the intended reader? (If this is the class teacher, it is up to him or her to state the degree of formality.)
b) what is the function of the piece of writing? (Clearly the tone needed for a student magazine will be more relaxed than that required for a formal report for a large organisation.)
2 Think about how you will paragraph the piece – compose the first sentence of each paragraph, and think about what information you will include in each.

Draft copy

You should now be ready to make a draft of the final piece.
1 On rough paper expand on the first sentences you have for each paragraph.
2 Neatness is not essential – so delete and add material as you think appropriate.
3 Ensure that information is set out in the correct order.

Proof-read

1 Re-read the draft once it is complete to check that it reads clearly and fluently.
2 Check spelling and grammar.

Layout

Once you are satisfied with the draft, you can copy out the finished piece.
1 Leave margins at the top and bottom and at both sides – this gives a neat appearance and space for comments if the piece is to be marked.
2 Each paragraph should be separated by a gap of one line.
3 Use only one side of the paper and number each page.
4 Write neatly or type if you can.

Proof-read again

Proof-read the final copy – this is your last chance to correct any mistakes.

  Language Guidelines © 1990 ALBSU. Published by Hodder & Stoughton.

It should be pointed out at this stage that not all the pieces of extended work that students do need to be in the written form. Students should be given the opportunity to present work in a variety of forms. Some students feel intimidated when doing written work and although they know all the relevant bits of information, fail to express them adequately.

As an alternative to extended pieces of writing, let students present their information by means of a short talk or by making a cassette tape or video. This can be done individually or in small groups. All the group members can collaborate in the collection of materials and determining the final structure of the talk or tape. Students could illustrate their talk or tape with slides, realia or role play.

The amount of time needed for production and presentation is obviously more than that for a straight piece of writing but it is surprising how keenly motivated students become so that they are willing to do additional work in their own time.

PROJECTS

A project is an extensive piece of work which entails a variety of methods of collecting and collating information and provides an ideal opportunity to integrate all the language skills, especially if the project is compiled by a small group of students.

But projects shouldn't be regarded as a catch-all for language skills. Each of the skills needed should be dealt with independently at first and gradually built upon and integrated. A project, therefore, should only be set once you are satisfied that the students have the individual skills they will need to complete it adequately.

Choosing a project title

When giving students a project, make sure that the title is not too vague (Shopping) nor too extensive (Transport throughout the world). 'Credit Cards' and 'Britain's Railways' would provide better titles since each is broad enough to provide scope and flexibility, yet within each of these subjects it is possible to identify specific topics for research sources. Both these subjects could be dealt with by giving a brief overview and then selecting a particular topic to present in greater detail. It may help students if, as well as a main title, various sub-topics are listed. They can then select ones that they are interested in or feel that they can cope with. But, if possible, students should be encouraged to choose their own sub-topics (though these should be submitted for approval before they begin their research).

The sub-topics could be such things as:

■ Credit Cards: Applying for a credit card.
                           How the credit card system operates.
                           The advantages and disadvantages of credit cards.
                           A case study of someone who got into debt through using credit cards.

■ Britain's Railways: The types of rolling stock used on the railways.
The freight network.
The channel tunnel.
A day in the life of a station master/mistress.

Part of the value of projects is that they allow flexibility so that when students show a particular interest in a topic, they can pursue this within their overall brief. This flexibility also allows for the different abilities within a classroom, and students can use those language skills which they feel happiest with. For example, a student may not feel very confident about his or her writing skills but may be good at oral communication. He or she could go out with a tape recorder and conduct interviews with local store managers, the Citizens Advice Bureau, railway employees, commuters, etc. (having first obtained their permission by letter or phone, of course).

Whilst students should be encouraged to obtain their research materials in a variety of ways and from a variety of sources, care must be taken that they do not antagonise people in the local community. (Project work can turn out to be an exercise in public relations for a school, college or training agency.) Most people who work for commercial organisations are only too willing to help students but their time is limited and they have other things to do. They will readily give advice, information, documents and brochures to one student but are less co-operative if asked to do so frequently. If source material is likely to be needed by many students, then it is better that once a few copies have been obtained, these are kept in a central resource bank. This should be kept up to date and replenished when stocks run low. Most large organisations will supply quantities of leaflets, brochures, magazines which are suitable for student use and some even produce special packs for schools and colleges (a list of these is included at the back of the book). Also, be on the look-out for suitable magazine and newspaper articles which can be added to the resource bank.

BASIC SKILLS

You may decide to refer any students who have lots of problems with their basic writing skills to whatever specialist unit your school or college has. However, it is possible and preferable to deal with simple errors in basic writing skills in the classroom. Most errors can be sorted out quickly, and remedies will have a greater impact if they are dealt with in the context of the situation in which they occur.

An ideal situation would be to have someone with specialist knowledge in basic skills to work alongside you in the classroom, but this is rarely possible. Help with basic skills will, therefore, have to be given by you.

BASIC SKILLS CHECKLIST

Spelling

1 Keep your own spelling book – each time you come across a new word that you are likely to need for your course, enter it in your book. If you enter the words in alphabetical order by their first letter, you will always have an easy and simple way of checking your spelling. Abbreviations and special terms can also be kept in this book.

2 Buy a small dictionary so that you can check the spellings of everyday words. This is in addition to your spelling book since many of the specialist words that occur in your course may not be included in a small dictionary.

3 Try to learn some of the spelling rules or invent your own method of remembering how to spell a word.

> e.g. hidden words: re*hear*sal, or*chest*ra
> jingles: *I* to the *end* will be a fr*iend*
> contrasts: station*e*ry includes *e*nvelopes, station*a*ry is st*a*nding still
> adapt pronunciation: parl*i*ament, lett*u*ce, We*d*nesday
> acronyms: CHEF – *C*ooks *H*ate *E*ggy *F*ingers

4 Always re-read your written work to check for spelling mistakes or get a friend to check it for you.

Punctuation

Try to learn some of the punctuation rules. (Mistakes are most often made on when to use the apostrophe and when to use capital letters.)

Handwriting

If you hand in written work or intend to keep it for future use, make sure your handwriting is neat:
- it is easier for other people to understand
- it is easier for you to re-read when you revise or need to look up information
- there is evidence that better marks are awarded in exams for papers that have been written in good legible handwriting

It is not possible to deal adequately with all the issues of basic skills within this book and, as there are already many excellent books available, it is better that you refer to some of these. A brief list of a few that I have found useful is included in the Reading List on page 69. Most of them are suitable for students to use and some include practice exercises.

External Exams

The language used for examinations and assignments has its own particular style and vocabulary. Students often have difficulty understanding what is expected of them. A recent Examiner's report from City and Guilds said:

'This year it would appear candidates have little understanding of what is meant by Concise, List, State and Describe.'

You will need to prepare your students for the type of language that they will encounter when doing exams and externally set assignments.

The first thing to do is to look at a selection of exams and assignments that students have had to do in the past. Look for any words or phrases that may cause difficulty. The main problems arise from those words that tell students what they have to do, e.g. express, define, indicate, determine. Sometimes the students are being asked to do more or less the same thing but it has been said in a different way so that the question paper does not become repetitious.

The extract from the City and Guilds leaflet on the next page is useful in trying to explain what some of the words which are used in exams and assignments mean. However, even their explanations are sometimes difficult to understand. Giving out the leaflet is not really adequate since many students merely put the leaflet in their bags or cases and never look at it again. What the students need is some practice at carrying out these instructions.

Ideally, students should be given short practice assignments which concentrate on a specific instruction word. Allowing for time to do this, however, is not always possible due to the demands of the main course work. Fortunately, many courses now involve continuous assessment, so students are doing tests and assignments throughout the year. As some of these tests and assignments are set internally, they can be used to introduce students to those instruction words that often cause difficulty.

Having determined which instruction words occur in external exams and assignments, make sure that these are included in your own tests and assignments. After handing out a test or assignment, go through the instructions to make sure the students understand exactly what is required. This will prepare them for external testing and also give an indication, at an early stage, which instruction words are not fully understood by your students.

This same procedure should also be followed for any other words or phrases that might cause problems.

e.g. What is the *principal* reason for wearing low heeled shoes for food service?

What are the chief *factors* that affect the absorption of fat when deep frying food?

What are the three *elements* of costing?

- Look for instruction words in the question such as 'describe' and 'explain'. These tell you the type of answer to give. Common instruction words are

List/Name	Give list or name facts required rather than sentences
State	Give the relevant fact(s) briefly and to the point
Describe/Detail	Give a full acount with examples of the procedure, term etc specified in the question
Outline	Briefly give all the essential points
Compare/Contrast	Point out similarities and differences, advantages and disadvantages, of the items mentioned in the question
Define	Give the exact meaning (eg. of a term, principle, procedure)
What is meant by . . . ?	More than just define – give a definition but go on to give some explanation and discuss its significance and limitations
Explain why . . .	Give the reason(s) for
Sketch	Do a freehand drawing
Draw	Do a fine-line-ruled drawing – to scale if required.

PRODUCING MATERIALS

WORKSHEETS AND HANDOUTS

There are many good textbooks available which cover the information required for a particular course and these often include exercises which check and reinforce students' understanding or provide stimuli for supplementary activities. But no matter how good a textbook is, it cannot cater for the mixture of abilities within a classroom or meet the demands of a constantly changing curriculum. There will be times when teachers have to produce their own handouts and worksheets. These are some points worth bearing in mind:

■ When devising handouts and worksheets, try to get a colleague to devise them with you or at least check and evaluate them when they are completed.

■ When giving out a worksheet or handout, explain what is required of the students, so that they know what they are expected to do.

■ Worksheets should always be given out before the activity to which they relate. The students are then aware of what information they are expected to look or listen for.

■ Continually evaluate worksheets and handouts to see if they need to be amended to make them more effective. Observe how students cope with them and listen to their comments. If there are any parts that they find particularly difficult, think of ways that might make them easier to understand.

■ In order to accommodate different abilities, devise preparatory worksheets for less able students and extended activities for the more able.

On the next page is a checklist for preparing worksheets and handouts. Task Sheets 35–39 give sample worksheets and handouts to illustrate the points made.

T A S K

Look at a selection of worksheets and handouts and, using the checklist as a guide, evaluate their good points and their bad points.
Try to think about how they might be improved.
Would you need to have a preparatory worksheet for any of them?
Could any of the sheets be supplemented with extended activities?

TASK SHEETS: 4–8, 13–31, 35–39

There are several points which you ought to remember when making a handout or worksheet, though you may not need to include all those listed below.

1 Language – think about the level of language that is suitable for your students. Read through the section on Reading for guidance on assessing materials.

  a) Keep it simple – use short sentences.
  b) Apart from technical words, try to use simple everyday words.
  c) Don't put too much information on a page.
  d) Avoid ambiguity.
  e) If the students are expected to write new or difficult words, set them out at the bottom of the sheet. This will avoid spelling errors.
  f) Keep instructions clear and simple.
  g) Only put one instruction per line.
  h) Put instructions in temporal order.
   e.g. Switch off the electricity before removing lid
   NOT
   Before removing lid, switch off the electricity.

2 Quality – students are more likely to take notice of a worksheet or handout if it has a 'professional' look to it.

  a) Give the worksheet or handout a title.
  b) Type it out or print it neatly in lower case letters, not capital letters.
  c) Leave space round the text.
  d) Leave space round illustrations, graphs, maps, charts, etc.
  e) Avoid large areas of uninterrupted print.
  f) Set your text out in short paragraphs.
  g) For large areas of text, use double or triple columns.

3 Construction – apart from the points above, there are other ways of setting out a worksheet or handout so that they are easier for students to read.

  a) Always put instructions first.
  b) Use different styles and sizes of lettering to highlight parts of the sheet.
  c) Use boxes to distinguish between certain features.
  d) Underline especially important parts of the text.
  e) If possible, try to use different colours for highlighting or distinguishing between features.
  f) Number or letter points but don't use too many. If you have a long list, mark them off with an asterisk or dash.
  g) Un-numbered lists should be set out in small groups of approximately five items which are separated by a space.
  h) If possible, try to make the worksheet flexible so that you can produce different versions to suit students with different abilities.
  i) Always include an illustration of some sort even if it does not relate directly to the text.
  j) Try to make illustrations amusing.

4 Variety – students will be more interested if they are given a wide variety of different types of worksheets and handouts.

  a) Try to use a variety of learning techniques. Some students learn better from one form than another.
  b) Don't always confine your students to working in the classroom. Give them work that requires the use of a variety of source materials.
  c) Don't always confine your students to written activities. Work can be presented in oral and graphic forms through the use of role play, short talks, cassette recorder, video or cartoon strip.

Language Guidelines © 1990 ALBSU. Published by Hodder & Stoughton.

PHOTOCOPYING

For some handouts or worksheets it may be necessary to photocopy materials from various sources. This should be all right providing that the quality of the text is not impaired. Some commercial publications permit photocopying and will usually state so. For all other commercial publications permission is needed. This will usually be granted freely providing the material is used only in the classroom. To get permission, you will need to tell the publisher:

- the name of the book or journal
- the name of the author, if known
- the date of publication
- the length of the extract you want to photocopy
- details of any diagrams or illustrations
- the page number
- what you intend to use the extract for

Points to remember

- Small or poor handwriting or print becomes even harder to read when photocopied.
- Newspaper print is difficult to photocopy. Experiment with the copier as there can be variation in quality from one copy to another. When you have a 'good' copy, use that as your master copy.
- Don't reduce materials from magazines, books, etc. – small print is hard to read.
- If students only need a bit of information from the page of a book, blank out those parts that they don't need to read. Try to arrange it so that the text they are to read comes in the centre of the page in the handout.
- Materials printed in black on a white background will photocopy best. Any other combination of colours will give poorer quality copies.

FURTHER READING

A Language for Life, Bullock Report (HMSO, 1975)

Language Across the Curriculum, Michael Marland (Heinemann, 1977)

Learning from the Written Word, Eric Lunzer and Keith Gardener (Oliver & Boyd, 1984)

Teaching Literacy and Numeracy to Craft Students, (ALBSU, 1983)

Communicating in the Classroom, (ed.) Clive Sutton (Hodder and Stoughton, 1981)

From Communication to Curriculum, Douglas Barnes (Penguin, 1976)

Reading, Frank Smith (Cambridge University Press, 1986)

Writing and the Writer, Frank Smith (Heinemann, 1982)

Lipservice; the story of talk in schools, Pat Jones (Open University Press, 1988)

How to Produce Better Worksheets, Robin Lloyd-Jones (Hutchinson, 1986)

How to Study, Francis Cary (Macmillan, 1985)

Books on Basic Skills

Handling Language 1, John Davis (Stanley Thornes, 1990)

Handling Language 2, John Davis (Stanley Thornes, 1990)

Handling Spelling, John Davis (Hutchinson, 1985)

Checkbooks: Punctuation, Phillip Payne (Hutchinson, 1983)

Checkbooks: Spelling, Martin Tucker (Hutchinson, 1984)

Spelling Matters, Bernard R. Sadler (Edward Arnold, 1982)

Punctuation in its Place, Don Shiach (Hodder and Stoughton, 1984)

Steps to Spelling, Don Shiach (Hodder and Stoughton, 1984)

Grammar Matters, Don Shiach (Hodder and Stoughton, 1985)

Nelson Grammar Books 1–5, Denis and Helen Ballance (Nelson, 1979)

Teaching the Basic Skills, Dan Smedley (Methuen, 1983)

An Introduction to Literacy Teaching (ALBSU, 1980)

Helping Adults to Spell (ALBSU, 1977)

Although designed primarily to teach English to speakers of other languages, the following books can be used in general language development. These books are particularly useful for illustrating the various language styles used in technical and academic writing.

Write Ideas, Glendinning & Mantell (Longman, 1983)

Basic Technical English, Comfort, Hick, Savage (Oxford University Press, 1983)

Writing through Pictures, J. B. Heaton (Longman, 1986)

Workshop English, Suzi Wells (Heinemann, 1985)

Patterns of Fact, Kennedy and Hunston (Edward Arnold, 1982)

English in Context, P. L. McEldowney (Nelson, 1982)

Organisations who supply materials suitable for project work

Advertising Standards Authority, Brook House, 2–16 Torrington Place, London WC1E 7HN.

Board of Inland Revenue, Education Service, PO Box 20, Wetherby, West Yorks LS23 7EH.

British Insurance Association, Alderman House, Queen Street, London EC4N 1TU.

BP Education Service, PO Box 5, Wetherby, West Yorks, LS23 7EH.

British Rail Education Service, PO Box 10, Wetherby, West Yorks, LS23 6YY.

British Telecom Education Service, Room 417, 2–12 Gresham Street, London EC2V 7AG.

Countryside Commission, John Dower House, Crescent Place, Cheltenham, GL50 3RA.

Department of Health and Social Security, 286 Euston Road, London NW1.

Institute of Petroleum Education Service, 61 New Cavendish Street, London W1M 8AR.

Post Office, Schools Officer, Room 127, 22–25 Finsbury Square, London EC2A 1PH.

Royal Society for the Prevention of Accidents, Cannon House, The Priory, Queensway, Birmingham B4 6BS.

National Dairy Council, Education Dept., National Dairy Centre, 5–7 John Princes Street, London W1M 0AP.

The Stock Exchange, Information and Press Department, The Stock Exchange, London EC2N 1HP.

A more comprehensive list can be found in *Treasure Chest for Teachers*. A copy should be available for reference in your local library or it can be obtained from:

> The Teacher Publishing Co., Ltd.,
> Derbyshire House,
> Lower Street,
> Kettering,
> Northamptonshire,
> NN16 8BB.

TASK
SHEETS

Assessing Materials

Passage A

Great masses of warm air and cold air move through the atmosphere all the time. Where a mass of warm air meets a mass of cold air the weather changes. The line where the two masses meet is called a front. When a mass of warm air overtakes a mass of cold air there is a warm front. The warm air is lighter than the cold air. It rises slowly over the cold air. As it rises clouds form and rain falls. When cold air overtakes a mass of warm air there is a cold front. The cold air burrows[100] under the warm air and pushes it up. Clouds form and often heavy rain falls. There may even be thunderstorms.

(from *Weather*, Macdonald First Library)

Passage B

The sensitivity of cloze items to the constraint outside the sentence was examined using a sample of 70 students from a Further Education College. Responses to cloze items in natural passages were superior to identical items in passages where the sentence order had been randomised in an attempt to destroy the intersentential constraint. No differences were found concerning the relative sensitivity to function or content words to intersentential constraint. Contrary to some previous findings, relevant context was found to have an effect on particular items, as the positioning of items at the end of natural passages did facilitate their prediction.[100] The natural passages also proved to be a much more valid test of reading comprehension than the modified order one.

(from *Journal of Research in Reading*, Vol. 7, No. 2)

Passage C

First cut notches in the head in which to fit the vertical studs which should be about 2 feet apart, which should make fixing the building boards easy. (At this stage you will have to decide where the door is going to be fixed, and allow an appropriate space for it within the framework of horizontal studs.)

Do the same with the floor plate. Now screw the head to the ceiling (prod the plaster with a bradawl until you find the centre of a joist). The next joist should normally be 18 inches away. If the line of the new[100] partition runs across the joists you can fix it anywhere. If it runs parallel to the joists, then you are confined to moving the position of the partition until it comes under one.

(from the *Guardian*, 15 July 1989)

Passage D

Nicotine is a drug which affects the nervous system and the circulatory system. It can either increase or decrease the activity of the nervous system, depending on other conditions. In general, it acts as a stimulant by increasing the release of adrenaline. This speeds up the heart rate and increases blood pressure by causing constriction of many blood vessels. Nicotine also increases the tendency for fatty deposits to form inside blood vessels and causes blood to clot. These two events can lead to thrombosis (clotting of blood within blood vessels). Deaths from coronary (heart) thrombosis and cerebral (brain) thrombosis are[100] increasing and smoking is an important factor in this trend.

(from *GCSE Biology* by Green, Potter and Stout)

Insulation of buildings

As will be seen from Figure 5.4:

(a) The outer walls of modern buildings are composed of a double layer of brickwork separated by an air-space, forming *cavity walls*. The air-space, being a good insulator, diminishes heat loss through the walls of the building. (See Figure 5.5 showing methods of heat loss.)

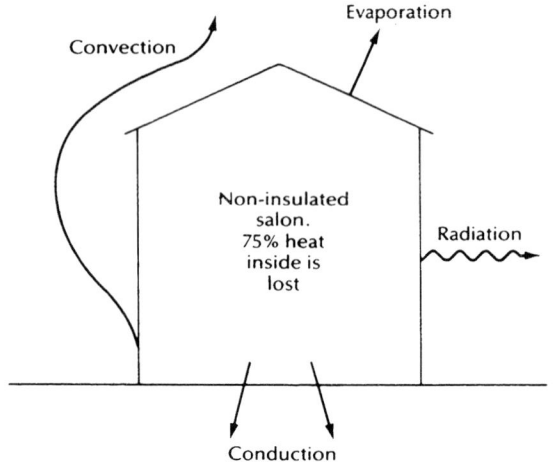

Figure 5.5 Heat Losses

(b) Windows are often double glazed, having an air-space between two sheets of glass; the air-space provides an insulation layer in the same manner as the cavity wall. Double glazing is also a useful means of sound insulation to prevent entry of noise into hotel rooms from busy streets.

(c) Attic, loft, and cellar spaces can be insulated with material laid across ceiling and floor joists. This prevents heat loss through ceilings and floors. Insulation material should not be placed beneath the attic storage tank but over it.

(d) Hot- and cold-water tanks and pipes are usually insulated or *lagged* to prevent heat loss and to prevent the pipes and tanks freezing in winter-time.

4. Cooking

(a) Double-bottom cake tins have air-spaces to prevent the cake bottom from burning.

(b) Earthenware is a poor heat conductor, consequently earthenware pots are used for *slow* cooking of pot roasts, daubes, and hotpots. Metalware containers are used for *rapid* cooking as in roasting.

(c) Food coatings such as pastry, sauces, and batters of various thickness act as *insulators* of heat, in the same way as the air-filled meringue does in baked alaska pudding.

CONVECTION

Convection in fluids is the process in which heat travels by the movement of the heated molecules.

CONVECTION IN LIQUIDS

Convection currents in liquids can be demonstrated visually by mixing aluminium powder with water in a beaker and gently heating the contents over a small flame, the aluminium powder particles will be seen to move. The apparatus which resembles a model hot-water system, can be used to demonstrate convection in liquids. The upper container or cistern is filled with coloured water; the boiler flask and connecting tubes contain cold water. When the boiler flask is heated, the coloured cold water descends to the boiler flask while the hot water rises to the upper container.

CONVECTION IN GASES

Convection currents in air can be shown by the chimney apparatus (Figure 5.6).

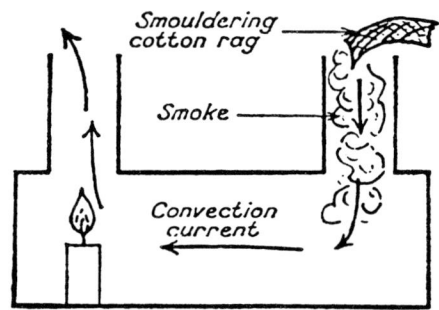

Figure 5.6 Convection in air

If the tissue wrapping paper from an orange is placed on a plate and lit with a match, the ash remaining will be seen to rise in the convection current produced by the burning paper.

Candle-lit table decorations which include revolving tinsel angels, stars, wheels, etc., depend on the rising convection currents from the burning candles.

APPLICATIONS OF CONVECTION CURRENTS

1. Food preparation

(a) Cooker ovens are heated by natural convection currents rising from the heater elements, the top part of the oven being hotter than the lower part. Similarly, refrigerators have convection currents of warm air rising towards the freezer unit and cold air descending (Figure 5.7). *Forced convection* is heat circulated by an electric fan.

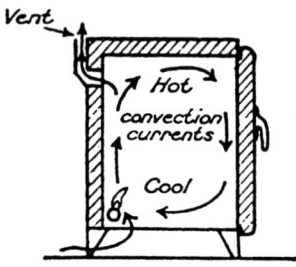

Figure 5.7 Natural convection in an oven

(b) The following cooking methods all depend on convection for heat transfer: boiling, baking, roasting, steaming, and deep-fat frying. The dry-heat methods of roasting and baking depend on the circulation of heat by convection and to a lesser extent on conduction of heat from the pan into the food.

Boiling, steaming, and deep-fat frying depend entirely on convection; they are quicker methods of cooking owing to the greater heat capacity and conducting powers of the water, fat, and steam compared to air.

2. Hot-water systems

The *low-pressure* hot-water system (Figure 5.8) is typical of the type fitted in many residences and often includes an electric immersion heater built into the hot-water cylinder. Water from the attic storage tank supplies the hot-water cylinder. This tank is at a higher level in order to provide the necessary head of water pressure to supply the system. The immersion heater is fitted into the base of the cylinder, so that the heated water rises to the top of the cylinder, allowing cold water to be drawn in for heating.

The expansion or safety pipe is a safety outlet to allow steam to escape from the system either into the attic

storage tank or directly through the roof into the air.

Heat radiators are often fitted as part of many hot-water systems.

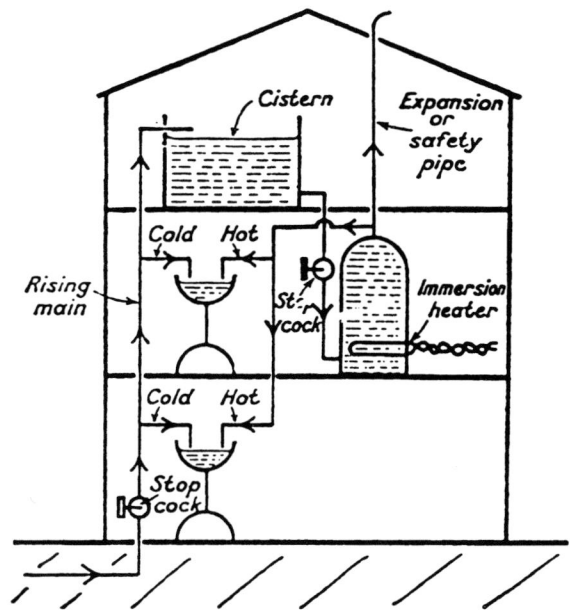

Figure 5.8 Hot-water system

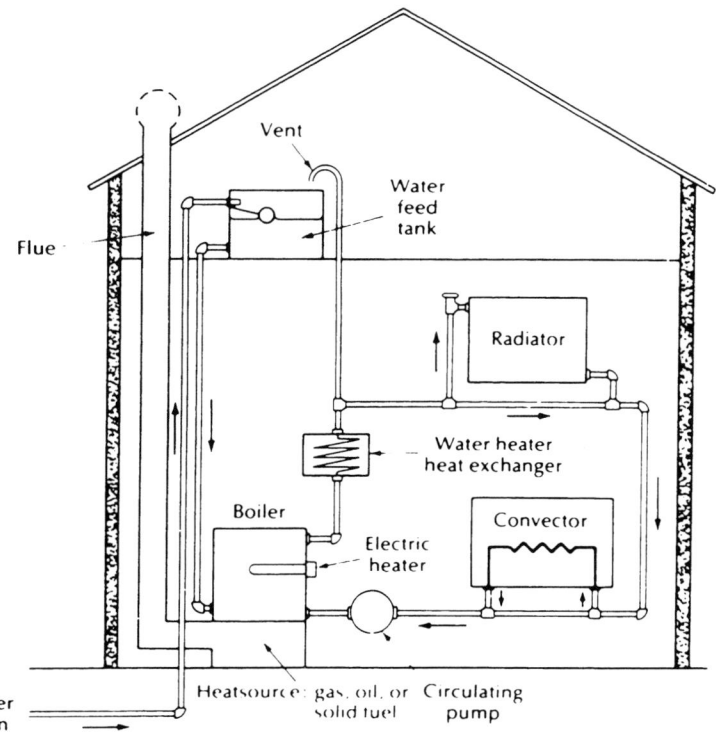

Figure 5.9 Central heating system

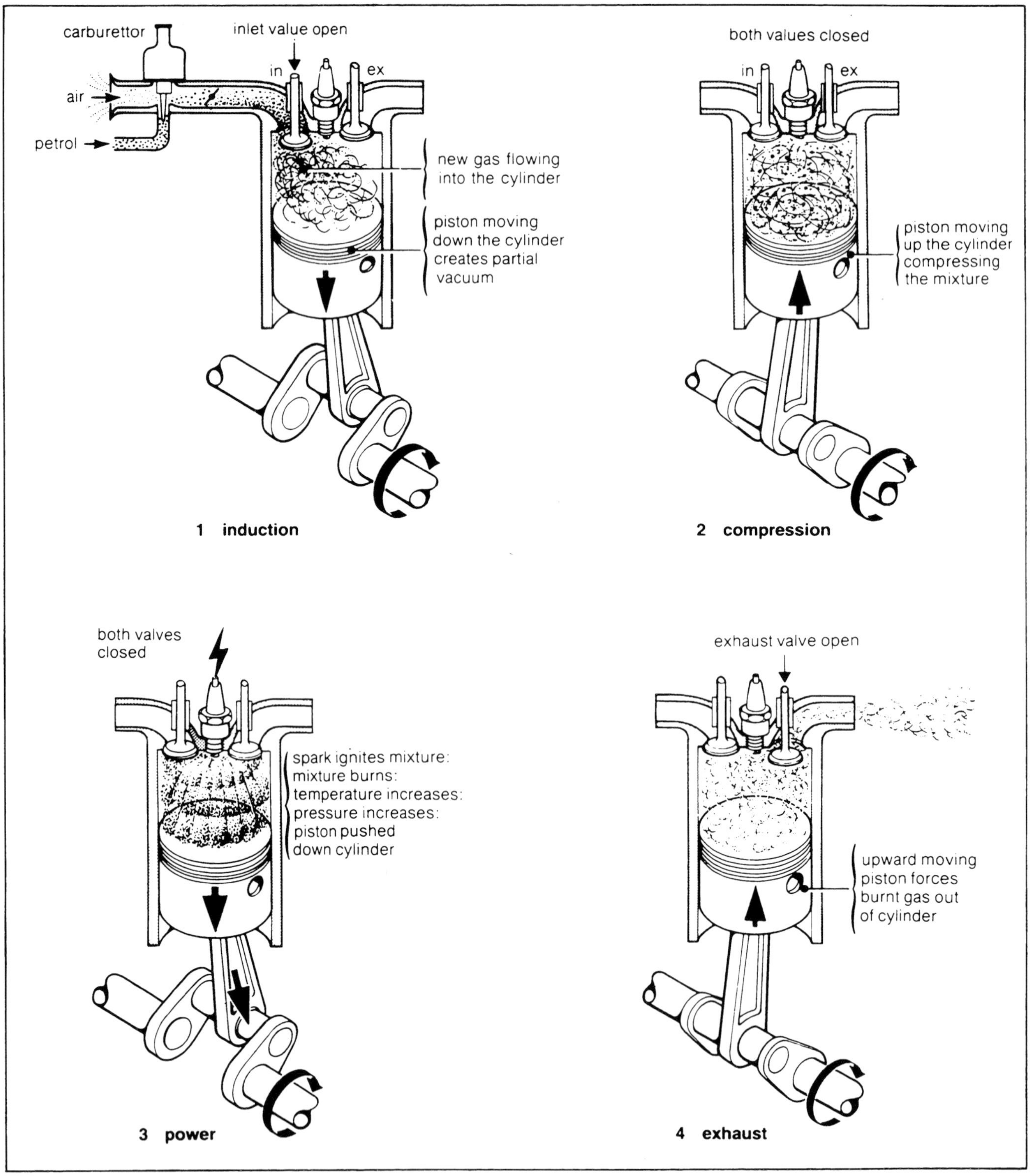

carburettor   inlet value open   both values closed

in   ex   in   ex

air →

petrol →

new gas flowing
into the cylinder

piston moving
down the cylinder
creates partial
vacuum

piston moving
up the cylinder
compressing
the mixture

1   induction

2   compression

both valves
closed

exhaust valve open

spark ignites mixture:
mixture burns:
temperature increases:
pressure increases:
piston pushed
down cylinder

upward moving
piston forces
burnt gas out
of cylinder

3   power

4   exhaust

13   Four-stroke cycle

[. . .]

Two main working cycles are used in a petrol engine
to allow the various operations to take place.

They are:
1 *Four-stroke cycle* – used on the majority of cars.
2 *Two-stroke cycle* – used on light motor cycles and garden machinery.

Four-stroke cycle

Credit for this operating cycle is given to the German engineer Dr N. A. Otto who took out a patent about 1875. Often called the '*Otto cycle*', the full sequence of events for one cylinder takes four strokes of the piston and involves two revolutions of the crankshaft.

Gas enters and leaves the cylinder through ports; an *inlet* port conveys the fresh petrol–air mixture into the cylinder and an *exhaust* port connects with an exhaust pipe which discharges the gas into the atmosphere.

Gas compression and expansion cannot take place if the ports are open, so each port is sealed by a *valve*. This valve only opens when gas flow through that particular port is required.

The four strokes of the working cycle are (13):

INDUCTION, COMPRESSION, POWER, EXHAUST

Starting with the piston at t.d.c., the operation comprises:

Induction

On the first stroke the piston moves down the cylinder; the inlet valve is open and the exhaust valve is closed.

The piston motion causes the pressure inside the cylinder to fall below the pressure of the atmosphere. This drop in pressure (often called a depression or partial vacuum) causes air to rush into the cylinder. Before entering the cylinder the air first passes through a *carburettor*: this meters out a set amount of petrol, mixes it with the air and controls the amount of petrol–air mixture that is to be supplied to the cylinder.

Compression

The piston moves up the cylinder and both valves are closed.

The gas cannot escape from the cylinder so the upward-moving piston compresses the mixture to produce a highly combustible charge.

Power

Both ports are closed and the piston moves down the cylinder. At the end of the compression stroke a spark, produced by a sparking plug screwed into the cylinder, ignites the mixture. Combustion takes place and the

high gas pressure forces the piston down the cylinder to provide the working stroke.

Exhaust

On this fourth stroke the piston moves up the cylinder towards t.d.c.; the exhaust port is open and the inlet port is closed.

Slight pressure caused by the piston movement pumps the burnt gas from the cylinder to prepare the engine for the next cycle.

The Otto cycle only has one working stroke in four, so a *flywheel* is needed to drive the engine during the period when the three 'non-working' strokes are taking place (14).

14 Flywheel

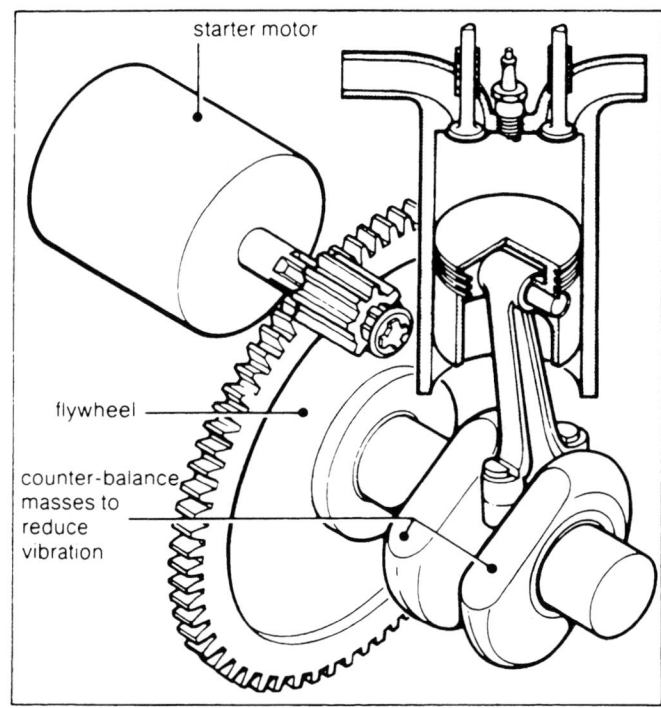

starter motor

flywheel

counter-balance masses to reduce vibration

Summary of the four-stroke Otto cycle

Cycle takes four strokes of the piston; two revolutions (720°) of the crankshaft.
Four-stroke sequence: induction, compression, power, exhaust.

	Piston direction	Inlet valve	Exhaust valve
Induction	down	open	closed
Compression	up	closed	closed
Power	down	closed	closed
Exhaust	up	closed	open

Complete the following notes:

MANUFACTURING OWN COMPONENTS

Advantages	Complete control of _____ , _____ and _____ .
	Can fit in with _____ _____ .
	Creates extra _____ and _____ .
	Can be advertised as made _____ by manufacturer.
Disadvantages	Additional cost of _____ , _____ and _____ .
	Less flexibility when demand _____ .
Other reasons	To use spare _____ .
	To avoid _____ .

THE MAKE OR BUY DECISION

One of the major production decisions that has to be taken in connection with certain components is whether they should be made in the manufacturer's own works or whether they should be bought in from an outside supplier.

There are a number of factors which need to be considered before a decision can be made. The advantages of making components internally are that the manufacturer has complete control over their quality, so ensuring finished products of acceptable standard, delivery times are completely in the hands of the production team as are the costs of manufacture, and additional earnings may be generated which may bring increased profit. It is thus possible to have components which relate precisely to production plans in quality, delivery and cost. Further, it may be a marketing advantage to be able to claim that a product is made in its entirety by the manufacturers of the complete product.

There are, however, some disadvantages. These include the need to finance this aspect of the product in regard to design costs, manpower and machine availability. In some cases additional machinery and work-people may be required. Having engaged in the manufacture of the components some flexibility in supply is lost. Where the market fluctuates it is easier to stop placing orders with outside suppliers than it is to run down production when there is a reduction in demand. Equally, should there be a sudden increase in demand it is more difficult to restart production to satisfy manufacturing requirements than it is to go into the market and buy.

Ideally, it is probably only advantageous to make components internally if there are spare facilities available, and then only if these facilities include appropriate design and development capabilities.

Finally, to an organisation with a social conscience a decision to make internally may be made on the grounds of avoiding redundancies among loyal employees should components be bought in from outside.

It is necessary to stress that production practices differ very widely from industry to industry and from enterprise to enterprise, particularly in relation to size and market. What is presented here is a general picture as an introduction to the subject of production and as a basis for understanding and appreciation of this function.

Language Guidelines © 1990 ALBSU. Published by Hodder & Stoughton.

Read through the extract from the *Barnsley Chronicle* and then decide which answer is correct to complete the statements.

1. The events took place on
   a) Monday
   b) Wednesday
   c) Friday

2. The mob was originally going to
   a) Denaby Main
   b) Wombwell
   c) Wath

3. The size of the mob eventually grew to
   a) 40
   b) 600
   c) 1500

4. When the mob reached the colliery they
   a) talked with the manager
   b) threw stones at the police
   c) attacked the office buildings

5. The coal fitters left
   a) in a brake van
   b) through the colliery yard
   c) after the fighting

COAL LOCK-OUT – TERRIBLE DEVASTATION AT WATH MAIN COLLIERY
SCENE AT A BREWERY – ARRIVAL OF MILITARY – RIOTERS ARRESTED

The scene in Wath and district on Wednesday was of such a character as almost to baffle description. Early in the day a mob, stated by some 600 strong, left Wombwell with, it was stated, the object of rioting at Denaby Main, where the Midland Railway Co. have been filling coal from the stock for a month. The men were armed with big cudgels, and were led by some desperadoes, one of whom carried a red flag, which he flaunted in the breeze. At Winterwell, about two miles on their journey, they halted and received certain information from the local miners, who grouped around, which caused them to have a council of war. (...) It was accordingly resolved to change the venue, so to speak, and the orders were given to proceed to Wath Main. It is stated that they stopped at several public houses and demanded and obtained drink, and that they forcibly entered several shops (...) Their forces were considerably increased as they went down the lane to the colliery, until they numbered fifteen hundred. (...) Leaving out the formality which they had observed at other collieries, namely, the parly with the managers on the unconscionable sin of coal filling, they proceeded to action, beginning by a general assault on the offices. Twelve policemen had come with the coal fitters to protect them in their work, and while their protagonists clamoured with their shovels in a brake van, and steamed away, the police made a rush for the colliery yard down a good gradient, and dealt some baton blows with good effect. The crowd retreated to the edge of the yard, and then commenced a savage attack with stones and stocks, against which the police were powerless, and had to fly to safety.

DISTURBANCES CONTINUE AND WAGONS ARE FIRED, THE ENGINE HOUSE SMASHED AND SET ON FIRE
While the fire was at its height, a body of 40 policemen headed by Supt. Hammond, of Rotherham, and Inspector Barrett of Mexbro', appeared upon the scene and sent the mob flying in all directions. Ten arrests were made [...]

(taken from the *Barnsley Chronicle*, 9 September 1893)

Read the article on the fog in
London and say whether these
eight statements are true or false.

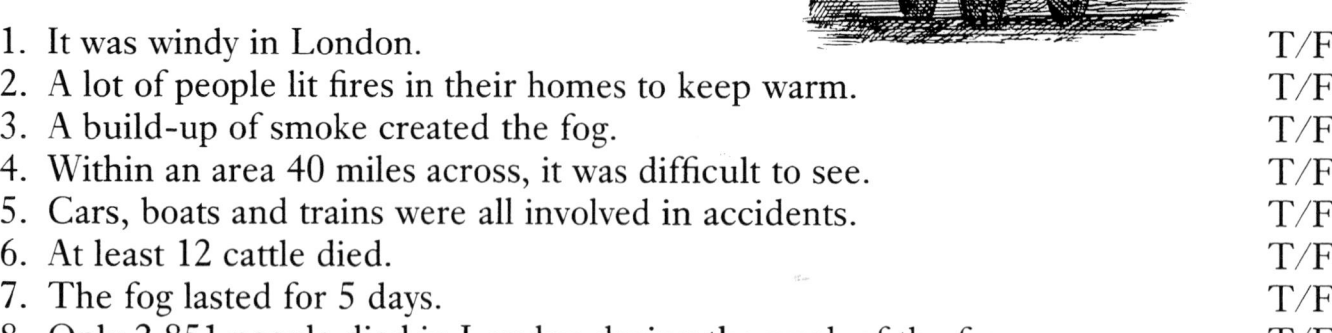

1. It was windy in London. — T/F
2. A lot of people lit fires in their homes to keep warm. — T/F
3. A build-up of smoke created the fog. — T/F
4. Within an area 40 miles across, it was difficult to see. — T/F
5. Cars, boats and trains were all involved in accidents. — T/F
6. At least 12 cattle died. — T/F
7. The fog lasted for 5 days. — T/F
8. Only 2,851 people died in London during the week of the fog. — T/F

London. A different picture unfolded in London on December 4, 1952. A high-pressure mass of cold air was moving from Europe across the English Channel toward the Thames Valley. Unlike the deep valleys of the Monongahela and Meuse topography, the broad stretch of the relatively low Thames Valley extends over many square miles. Because of cold temperatures and moist air, the Londoners' fireplaces were working overtime.

There was a practically complete cessation of air movement. For 5 days the city was engulfed in a heavy cloud of smoke, which condensed in the moisture of London's fog. Within a radius of 20 miles the smoke had rendered the atmosphere so opaque that there were collisions of automobiles and trains. A steam ferry collided with a vessel at anchor on the Thames. At Earls' Court, where a show of prize cattle was in progress, some 160 animals developed fast, labored breathing and fever. Among the dozen animals that were autopsied, inflammatory changes in the bronchial tree, pneumonia, and emphysema were found.

When the fog lifted, after 5 days, most Londoners had not as yet realized the seriousness of the disaster in terms of sickness and deaths in the population. During the week ending December 13, *2851 persons over the usual death rate had lost their lives; during the following weeks, another 1224 deaths were attributed to the fog.* Even today it is impossible to assess adequately the death toll caused by respiratory and heart diseases in the wake of this disaster.

In 1956, London was again the scene of a fog disaster. At that time, *there were about 1000 deaths above the usual rate*, although the fog lasted only 18 hours.

Basic woodworking joints

Complete the following list:

Joints in width type of joint	generally used for
butt joint	
	sheds
loose tongue	
	cladding, panelling, external doors, gates
tongue and groove; surface nailing secret nailing	

Joints in width

This type of joint enables narrow boards to be built up to cover large areas (floor boards, cladding, etc.), or built up to form wider boards for shelving, cabinet work, table tops, etc. Figure 158 shows a butt joint where the square edges of the pieces of timber are glued together.

Figure 159 is an improvement of the butt joint. Both sides are grooved out and a loose plywood tongue is inserted. It is mainly used for cabinet work and counter tops.

For flooring, a tongue and groove joint (T & G) is used. Figure 160 shows the section for surface nailing and Figure 161 for secret nailing (nailing through the tongue). Figure 162 shows tongued, grooved and vee-jointed boarding, (T, G & V or matchboarding). It is mainly used for cladding, panelling and external door or gate construction.

Another boarding used for cladding is shiplap. It is widely used for covering sheds, etc. See Figure 163.

Figure 158 *Butt joint*

Figure 159 *Loose tongue*

Figure 160 *Tongue and groove (T & G) boarding: surface nailing*

Figure 161 *T & G boarding: secret nailing*

Figure 162 *T, G & V jointed (matchboarding)*

Figure 163 *Shiplap boarding*

Turn to Chapter 4 of 'Carpentry and Joinery for Building and Craft Students' and make similar lists for the other main groups of joints.

Name the different layers that make up the epidermis, and label the diagram.

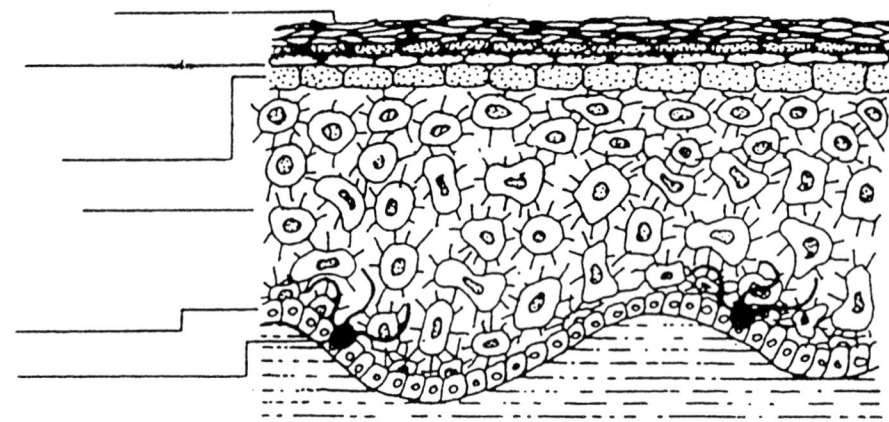

The Epidermis

The epidermis is composed of several layers of very small *cells*. On the outer surface the cells are dead and compressed into flat scale-like flakes made of the horny material *keratin*. These dead flakes form the cornified (horny) layer of the epidermis, and prevent water loss from the skin, apart from that lost by sweating. If the cornified layer is stripped off, water loss increases up to twenty times. Next comes a *lucid* (clear) layer, followed by a *granular* layer where the keratin is formed in the epidermal cells. These two layers which are only clearly visible in the thick skin of the sole of the foot and palm of the hand, form the transition zone between the outer dead cornified layer and the inner living dividing cells which form the *germinating* layer (stratum germinativum; Malpighian layer). The germinating layer consists of several rows of *prickle* cells and a single lowermost row of *basal* cells. The basal cells divide, cutting off new cells to the outside. The growth rate is greatest between midnight and 4 a.m., which may explain the term 'beauty sleep'. Ultra-violet rays and pressure or friction on the skin surface stimulate the basal cells to divide more rapidly.

These newly formed cells at first have fine threads connecting them to the cells around them, hence the name 'prickle' cells. As they are pushed towards the outside by new cells forming below, they become flatter. It takes between 40 and 56 days for a new cell produced by the basal layer to be pushed up to the skin surface.

The germinating layer contains the dark pigment *melanin*. All races contain some melanin in their skin, the darker the skin the greater the amount of melanin. The dark pigment absorbs harmful *ultra-violet* rays present in sunlight. The melanin is produced by large branched cells called *melanocytes* which lie among the cells of the basal layer. *Freckles* are due to the occurrence of a few very active melanocytes forming small dark areas which increase on exposure to sunlight. *Moles* are congenital pigmented growths of the epidermis which do not contain blood capillaries. Hairy moles are common on the face. Moles must not be interfered with as they can become cancerous and any increase in size of a mole should be reported to a doctor.

Facts about fat

There are two types of fat in your food . . .

SATURATED FATS . . . and UNSATURATED FATS

These include a special group called
POLYUNSATURATED FATS

There's a lot of evidence that eating too much fat can do us harm.

Fat is loaded with calories and eating too many calories will lead to overweight and obesity.

The main problem as far as your heart is concerned, is too much *saturated* fat.

Eating too much saturated fat tends to . . .

. . . increase the level of cholesterol in the blood

. . . increase the build up of cholesterol on the inside of the arteries, especially around the heart

. . . increase the risk of a complete blockage, causing a heart attack.

Front brake pads – inspection and renewal

1   Remove the wheel trim, slacken the wheel bolts and jack up the front of the car. Support the car on axle stands and remove the front roadwheels.

2   Inspect the thickness of the friction material on each pad. If any one is at or below the specified minimum, renew the pads as an axle set (four pads) in the following way.

3   Drive out the pad retaining pins by applying a suitable punch to their inboard ends. Be prepared for the pad tension springs to be released as the pins are driven out.

4   With the tension springs removed, withdraw the pads, one at a time from the caliper, using pliers if necessary (photos).

5   With the pads removed inspect the friction material for signs of oil or hydraulic fluid contamination, heavy scoring or cracking and for the security of the friction material on the metal backing. Renew all four pads if any one exhibits these conditions.

6   Brush away the dust and dirt from the caliper, piston and disc, but **do not** inhale as it is injurious to health.

7   Rotate the brake disc by hand and scrape away any rust and scale. Carefully inspect the entire surface of the disc and if there are any signs of cracks, deep scoring or abrasions, the disc must be renewed. Also inspect the caliper for signs of fluid leaks around the piston, corrosion or other damage. Renew the piston seals or the caliper body if necessary.

8   If new brake pads are being fitted it will be necessary to push the caliper piston fully into its bore to accommodate the new thicker pads. Using a flat bar such as a tyre lever or a large screwdriver, carefully lever the piston squarely into its bore as far as it will go. The action of depressing the piston will cause a quantity of hydraulic fluid to be returned to the master cylinder reservoir. Remove the reservoir filler cap and place absorbent rags around the master cylinder to collect any fluid that may overflow, or preferably syphon some fluid from the reservoir using a syringe.

9   Place the new pads in position in the caliper with the friction material against the disc.

10 Position the tension springs over the pads and drive in the retaining pins from the outside to the inside (photos).

11 Refit the roadwheels and lower the car to the ground.

12 Depress the footbrake several times to bring the piston into contact with the pads and centralise the caliper.

13 Top up the master cylinder reservoir if necessary and refit the filler cap. **Note:** *If new brake pads have been fitted, avoid unnecessary heavy braking for the first 120 miles (200 km).*

5.4A Removing the inboard pad

5.4B Removing the outboard pad

5.10A Position the tension springs against the pads ...

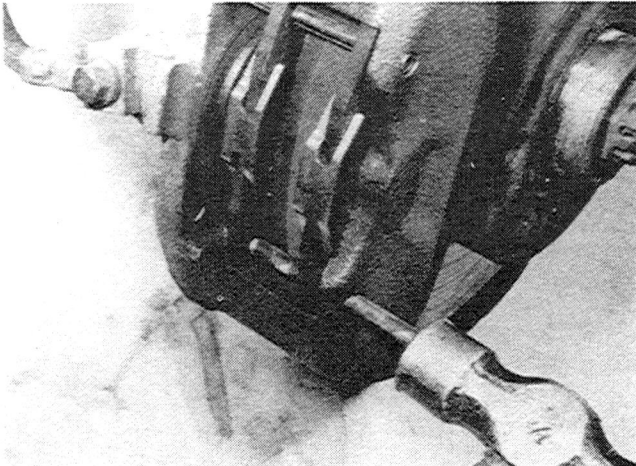

5.10B ... and drive in the retaining pins

The micrometer

On a modern micrometer the pitch of the screw thread is 0.5 mm, which means that one revolution of the screw moves it axially 0.5 mm. The screw is fixed to a graduated collar called the thimble (item 2 in Figure 47), which has 50 equal divisions on its circumference:

$$\therefore \text{ one division on the thimble} = \frac{0.5}{50} \text{ mm}$$

$$= 0.01 \text{ mm}$$

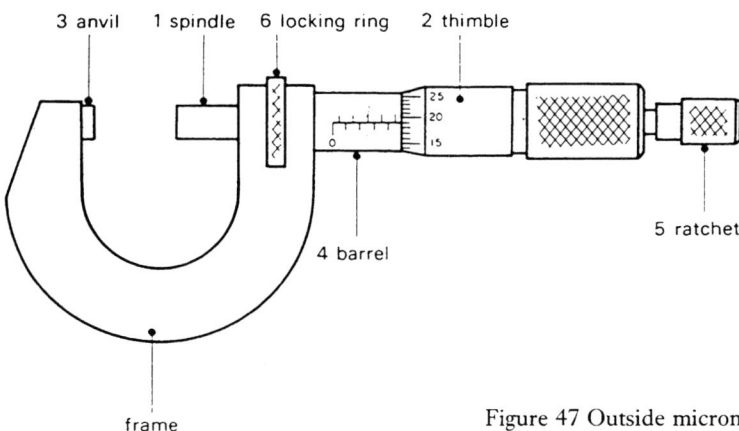

Figure 47 Outside micrometer

The basic components of the micrometer screw, that is the spindle (item 1 in Figure 47) and the thimble (item 2 in Figure 47) can be used in a variety of ways.

Before a micrometer is used to measure the size of a component it is necessary to zero the instrument. To do this the thimble is rotated until the two anvils are touching and the ratchet slips. At this point a reading is taken; this should read zero, i.e. the thimble should coincide with the zero reading on the barrel and the zero marking on the thimble coincide with the barrel datum marking. If the reading is not zero then the discrepancy should be allowed for in all further readings.

Figure 48 shows an outside micrometer being used to measure across the faces of a component; the component is placed between the anvil (item 3 in Figure 47) and the spindle (Figure 48).

The thimble, which is locked to the spindle, is turned until contact is just made with the component. A measurement is taken by noting the position of the thimble in terms of the graduations around its circumference and its position on the barrel (item 4 in Figure 47). A consistent degree of pressure or 'feel' is applied by the micrometer spindle on the component by a ratchet (item 5 in Figure 47), which is fitted to the end of the thimble. At a set pressure, the ratchet slips. At this setting the locking ring (item 6 in Figure 47) is tightened, and the reading taken. To take the reading, the number of divisions visible on the main barrel scale is first noted; every two divisions represent a spindle movement of 1 mm. Then the graduation on the circumference of the thimble that is adjacent to the barrel markings is noted. This reading is now added to the reading noted on the barrel.

For example, Figure 49 shows that eleven divisions on the barrel are visible; this means the spindle has moved 5.5 mm from its zero position. On the thimble the nineteenth graduation is adjacent to the barrel marking, thus:

the reading is 5.5 + (19 × 0.01) mm
        = 5.5 + 0.19 mm
        = 5.69 mm

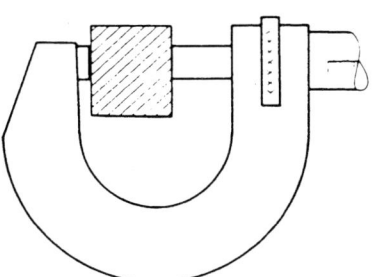

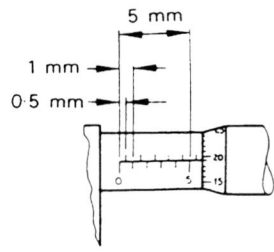

Figure 48 An outside micrometer being used to measure across flats

Figure 49 Micrometer reading

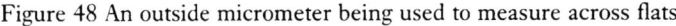

Natural stone

In recent years the use of natural stone as a facing material, or *cladding*, to buildings has to a great extent replaced the use of solid masonry blocks. The normal method is for thin stone facing slabs to be attached to brickwork or other backing, supported by a structural steel or reinforced concrete frame.

The geological classification of natural stone may be conveniently considered within three groups, according to the manner of its formation, namely *igneous*, *sedimentary* and *metamorphic*.

Igneous rocks

The igneous rocks were formed by the original cooling of the Earth's crust from its molten state (*magma*) and are also known as *primary* rocks.

Types of igneous rock   *Plutonic* rocks are those formed at considerable depth and are consequently coarse-grained. *Hypabyssal* rocks are those formed at intermediate depth, often by the cooling of volcanic magma which had flowed into fissures in the Earth's crust. They are typically of fine crystalline texture. *Volcanic* rocks are those formed at the surface of the Earth, by the rapid cooling of volcanic magma giving a very fine crystalline, or glassy, texture.

Igneous rocks are also classified according to silica content. Those containing more than 66% are termed *acid* and those with less than 52% *basic*. The remainder are termed *intermediate*.

Granites   It is common commercial practice to call any igneous rock used in building, a *granite*, and the term is even applied to some of the harder limestones, which are non-igneous. But strictly speaking, all true granites are plutonic rocks of acid character.

True granites may be distinguished from other igneous rocks by the fact that they are coarser grained (large crystals are visible without magnification) and generally of lighter colour, e.g. light grey.

Two examples of the many commercial 'granites' available are the *syenites* which are intermediate plutonic rocks of similar texture to true granites, but of a finer grain and darker in colour, and *basalts*, which are basic volcanic rocks of very fine, or glassy, texture, and almost black.

In general, *granites* are the strongest and most durable of all building stones, with very low porosity and water absorption, but they are the most difficult to work.

In addition to their value in heavy constructional and civil engineering work, many colourful granites are highly polished for use as a facing material, where they offer a not-inferior alternative to many polished marbles.

Sedimentary rocks

Sedimentary rocks are also known as *secondary* rocks. They were formed after cooling and solidification of the Earth's crust and their formation was by one of three agencies: mechanical, chemical and organic.

The *mechanical* formation of rocks resulted from the decomposition of the primary rocks by weathering and erosion. The detritus so produced was deposited over long periods to form successive layers which subsequently compacted to form a solid mass.

The *chemical* formation of rocks may have occurred by the precipitation of calcium carbonate (limestone) from water containing calcium bicarbonate in solution. It is this action which produces *stalactites* and *stalagmites* often found in caves in limestone regions.

The *organic* formation of rocks occurred as a result of the deposition of countless layers of minute sea organisms, plants or crustaceans. They can be of limestone or silica. Sedimentary rocks include sandstone and limestones.

Limestones   These are of calcium carbonate (*calcite*), magnesium carbonate (*magnesite*) or both (*dolomite*), usually together with 'impurities' such as iron oxides, sand or clay. Different limestones show wide variation in durability, and whereas the softer, more porous varieties, e.g. chalk, are usually unsuitable for most building work, some of the harder, more crystalline types, e.g. some *carboniferous* limestones, are similar in texture, density and strength to igneous rocks or marbles. The colour of limestones varies from white, grey, blue and pink to yellow.

Metamorphic rocks

The name *metamorphic* is given to rocks that have undergone a change from their original form by the action of pressure or high temperature, or both. The two important examples are *marble* and *slate*.

Marble   True marble is a recrystallized metamorphic form of limestone. Commercially, however, most limestones which are sufficiently hard to take a polish are classified as marbles. The presence of coloured veins in marbles is due to impurities, such as iron oxides, and can result in a highly attractive appearance.

Slate   Slates are metamorphic forms of clays and shales formed from the detritus of weathered igneous rocks; or they can also consist of metamorphosed volcanic dust.

Slates have a laminated structure and are easily split into thin slabs which have been widely used in the past as a roof covering because they are highly impervious. Slate is now widely used as cladding and will take a polish.

Symbols

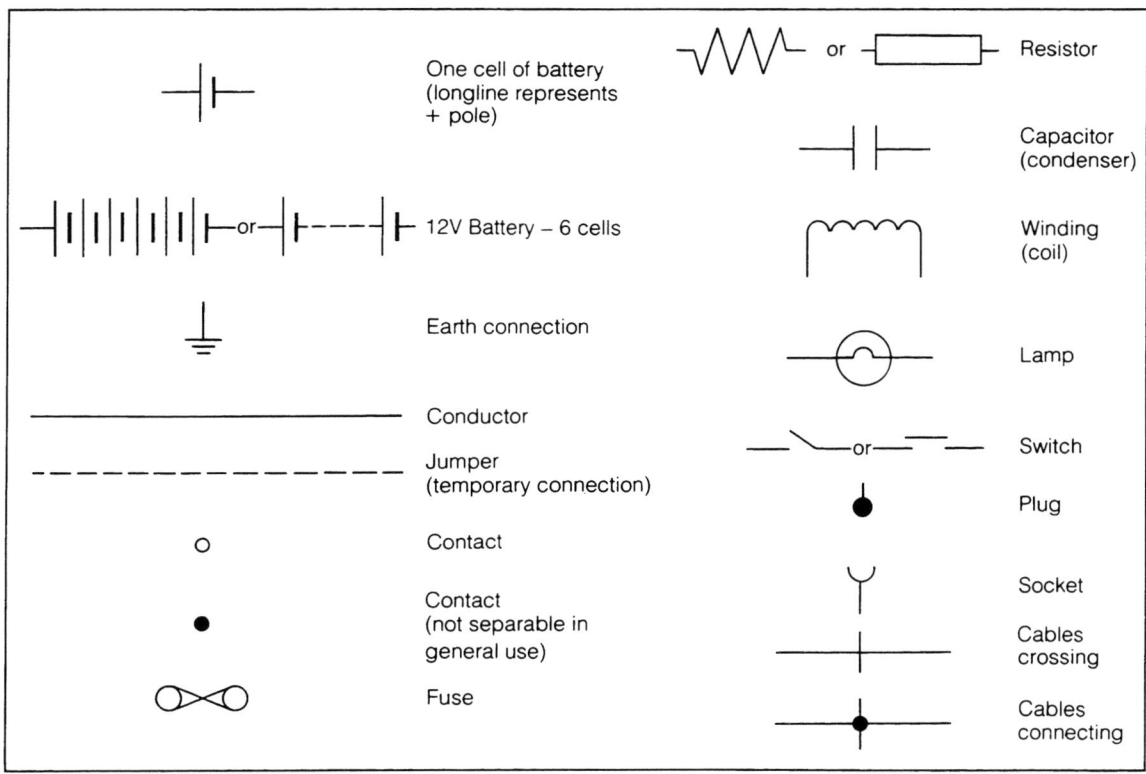

To save time and space when drawing electrical circuits, it is usual to represent the various electrical items by symbols. Some of the more common items are shown above. Look at these and then answer the following questions.

What is the symbol for an earth connection?

What is the symbol for a socket?

What is the symbol for a fuse?

What are the four items shown in this diagram?

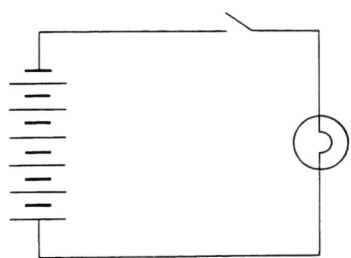

Painting on the Outside

Sally is very keen to do all the jobs about the house. Today she is going to do some painting outside. On task sheet 15 you will see some drawings of the things she is going to paint. Using the chart below, write down the types of paint she will be able to use for each of the different surfaces. She will need a primer (where applicable), an undercoat and a finish.

Surfaces	FILLERS, SEALERS AND PRIMERS												UNDER-COATS			FINISHES																	VARNISHES AND STAINS							Surfaces
	Shellac knotting	Bleach	Alkyd wood primer	Aluminium wood primer	Emulsion wood primer	Rubber based primer	Zinc phosphate	Zinc chromate	Etch primer	Zinc rich primer	Masonry sealer	Wood filler	Alkyd undercoat	Epoxy undercoat	Polyurethane undercoat	Alkyd gloss	Alkyd dripless	Emulsion vinyl	Alkyd eggshell	Emulsion exterior	Textured emulsion	Emulsion stone finish	Rubber based paint	Epoxy paint 2 pack	Polyurethane paint 1 pack	Polyurethane paint 2 pack	Cement paint	Floor paint	Metallic paint	Masonry paint	Fire retardant paint	Silicone water repellent	Alkyd varnish	Spar varnish	Polyurethane varnish	Moisture cured urethane	Oil stain	Spirit stain	Water stain	
Raw wood																																								**Raw wood**
Softwood	•	•	•	•	•							•	•	•	•	•	•		•				•	•	•					•			•	•	•	•	•	•	•	Softwood
Hardwood	•	•		•	•							•	•	•	•	•	•		•				•	•	•					•			•	•	•	•	•	•	•	Hardwood
Plywood			•	•	•							•	•	•	•	•	•		•				•	•	•					•			•	•	•	•	•	•	•	Plywood
Hardboard			•		•							•	•	•	•	•	•	•	•				•							•			•	•						Hardboard
Raw masonry																																								**Raw masonry**
New plaster			•										•			•	•	•	•																					New plaster
Gypsum plaster			•										•				•	•																						Gypsum plaster
Concrete				•							•		•		•		•		•	•	•	•	•		•		•			•		•								Concrete
Cement render				•							•				•		•		•	•	•	•			•		•			•		•								Cement render
Brickwork				•							•		•		•		•	•	•	•	•	•	•		•		•			•		•								Brickwork
Asbestos sheet			•	•							•		•			•			•	•	•	•	•		•					•										Asbestos sheet
Concrete floors				•																				•				•			•									Concrete floors
Bare metal																																								**Bare metal**
Iron and steel					•	•	•	•		•			•	•	•	•	•		•				•	•	•				•											Iron and steel
Galvanized iron							•	•					•	•	•	•	•		•				•	•	•				•											Galvanized iron
Aluminium							•	•					•	•	•	•	•		•				•	•	•				•											Aluminium
Copper and bronze													•			•			•				•	•	•				•					•	•	•	•	•		Copper and bronze
Previous surface covering																																								**Previous surface covering**
Wallpaper					•								•	•																										Wallpaper
Canvas and hessian					•								•	•																•										Canvas and hessian
Polystyrene					•								•																											Polystyrene
Plastic													•			•	•		•										•			•		•						Plastic
Alkyd matt and eggshell[2]													•	•	•	•	•	•	•										•			•								Alkyd matt and eggshell[2]
Alkyd gloss[2]													•	•	•	•	•		•										•			•								Alkyd gloss[2]
Emulsion vinyl[1,2]					•								•	•	•	•	•	•	•										•				•							Emulsion vinyl[1,2]
Emulsion acrylic primer[1,2]					•								•	•	•	•	•	•	•	•									•				•							Emulsion acrylic primer[1,2]
Emulsion exterior[1,2]												•							•	•	•	•																		Emulsion exterior[1,2]
Emulsion stone finish[1]												•						•	•	•																				Emulsion stone finish[1]
Epoxy/Polyurethane 2 pack													•	•	•									•	•	•														Epoxy/Polyurethane paint 2 pack
Polyurethane gloss and varnish[2]													•	•	•	•	•		•						•								•	•	•	•				Polyurethane gloss and varnish[2]
Rubber-based paint				•																			•																	Rubber-based paint
Metallic paint					•								•	•	•	•	•												•											Metallic paint
Cement paint												•															•													Cement paint
Masonry paint				•															•	•	•	•																		Masonry paint
Wood preservative																																	•	•	•					Wood preservative
Wood stain		•	•										•	•	•	•	•		•				•	•	•		•		•	•			•	•	•	•	•			Wood stain

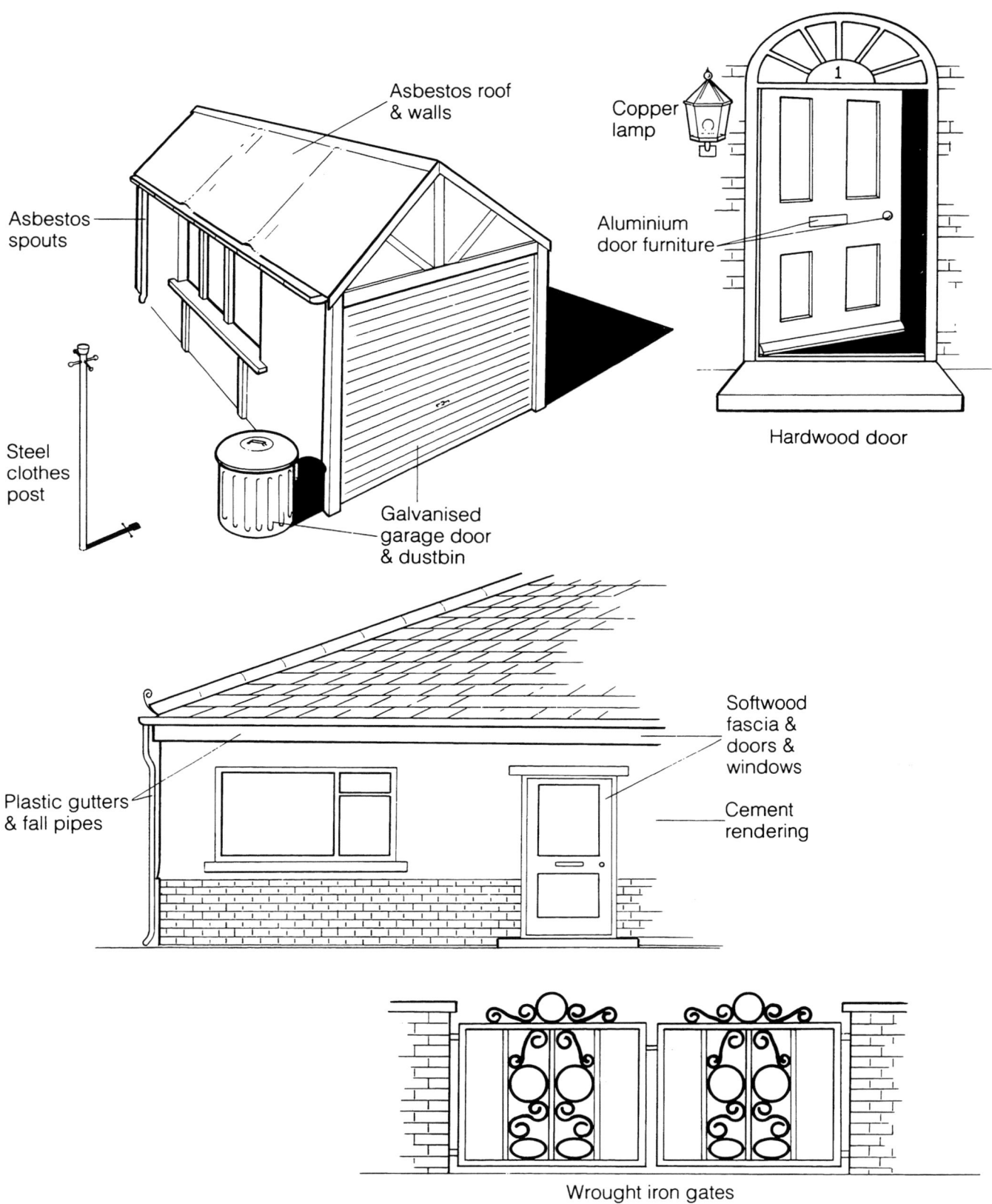

Asbestos roof & walls

Asbestos spouts

Steel clothes post

Galvanised garage door & dustbin

Copper lamp

Aluminium door furniture

Hardwood door

Plastic gutters & fall pipes

Softwood fascia & doors & windows

Cement rendering

Wrought iron gates

Spot the Difference

Levels of political activity 1979

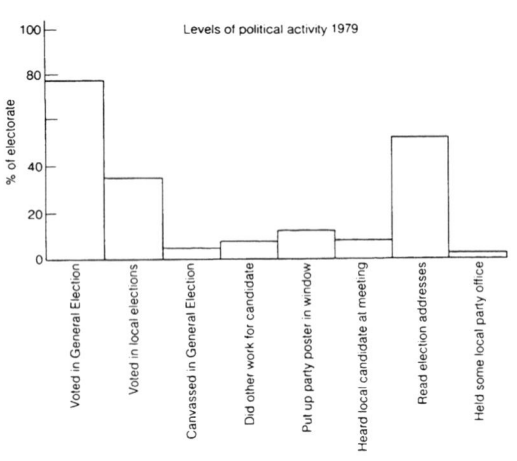

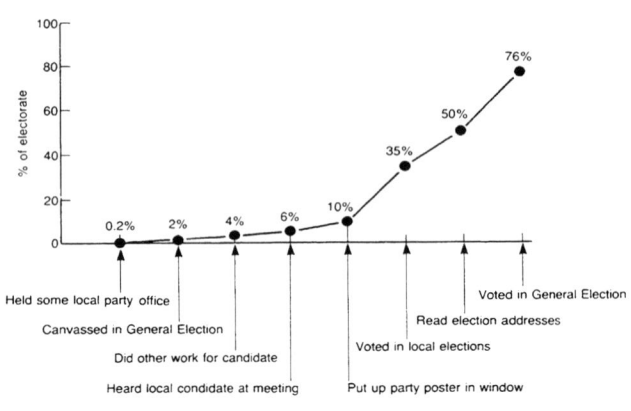

How the year's sales of a local department store are made up

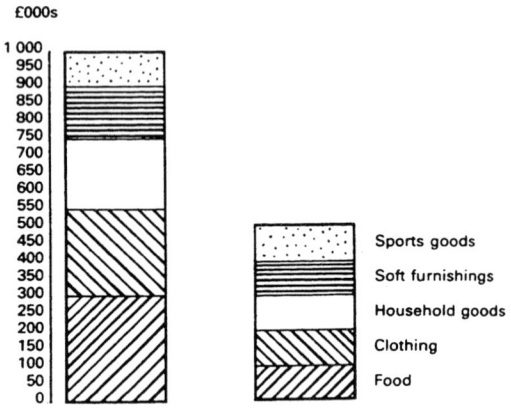

The Hasselblad 500C and 500C/M

1 Frame counter of film magazine.
2 Magazine latch.
3 Winding knob.
4 Locating mark for winding knob.
5 Time exposure lock.
6 Release for focusing hood and for magnifier.
7 Depth of field indicator.
8 Winding crank of magazine.
9 Magazine slide.
10 Focal plane mark.
11 Folding focusing hood.
12 Magnifier.
13 Shutter release with cable release socket.
14 Focusing mount of standard lens.
15 Shutter speed ring.
16 Transport signal of magazine.
17 Transport signal on camera body.
18 Exposure value and aperture setting lever.

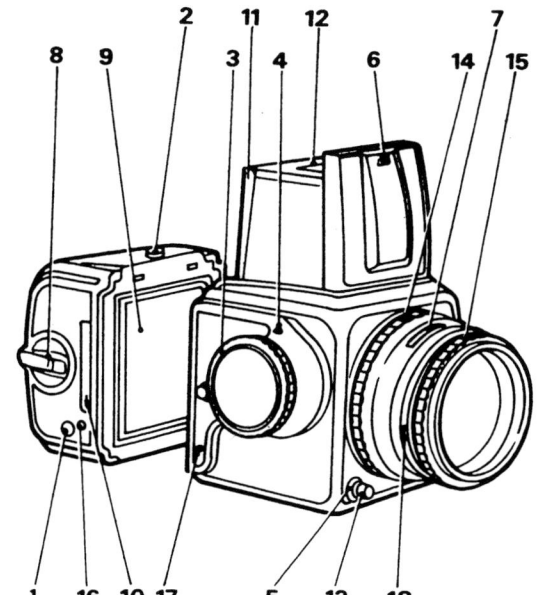

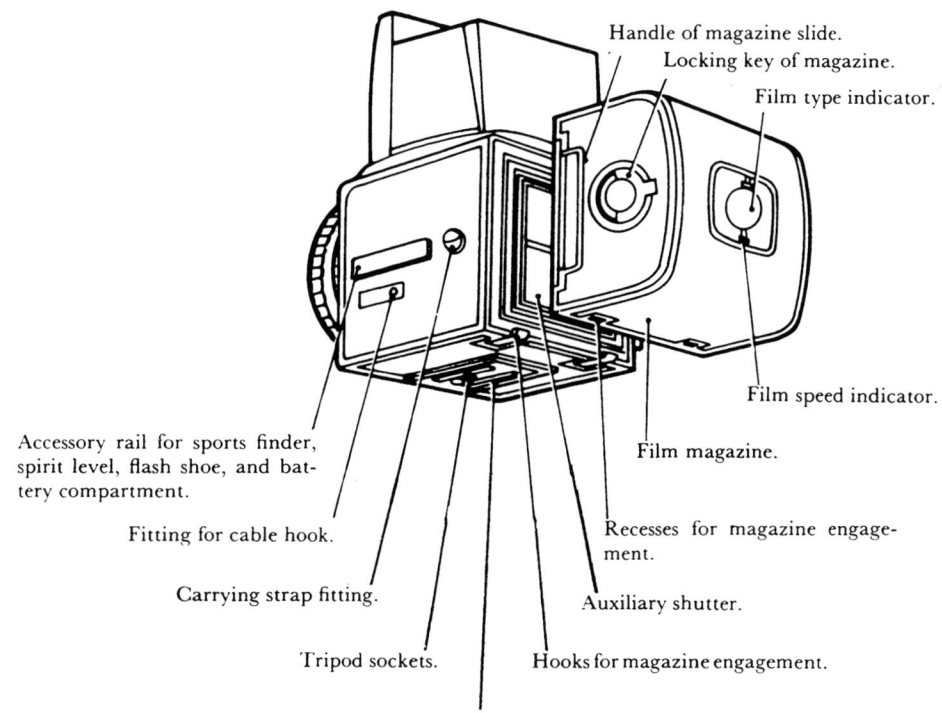

Handle of magazine slide.
Locking key of magazine.
Film type indicator.

Film speed indicator.

Film magazine.

Accessory rail for sports finder, spirit level, flash shoe, and battery compartment.

Recesses for magazine engagement.

Fitting for cable hook.

Auxiliary shutter.

Carrying strap fitting.

Hooks for magazine engagement.

Tripod sockets.

Baseplate for quick tripod coupling.

Choosing a book

You have been asked to look up the basic principles of hydraulic pressure. A quick glance at the shelf in the library shows that these books are a possible source of information. Which books would you choose to look at first?

Nuffield Physics, Pupils Text Year 1 (Longman, 1978)
Nuffield Physics, Pupils Text Year 2 (Longman, 1978)
Nuffield Physics, Pupils Text Year 3 (Longman, 1978)
Nuffield Physics, Pupils Text Year 4 (Longman, 1978)

The Physics of Vibrations and Waves, H J Pain (John Wiley, 1976)

Physics for Today and Tomorrow, Tom Duncan (John Murray, 1977)

Madam Curie, Robert Reid (Scientific Book Club, 1974)

Mysticism and the New Physics, Michael Talbot (Routledge, Kegan Paul)

Physics as a Liberal Art, James S Trefil (Pergamon, 1978)

Understanding Physics 1, D R Harrison (Heinemann, 1983)
Understanding Physics 2, D R Harrison (Heinemann, 1983)
Understanding Physics 3, D R Harrison (Heinemann, 1983)

Essential Physics, Kirkup, Murkett, Roe, Veasey (Pitman, 1983)

Technician Physical Science 1, R G Meadows (Cassells TEC Series, 1977)

Practical Physics at A Level, Trevor Cross (Collins, 1985)

A New Introduction to Physics, W Ashhurst (John Murray, 1971)

Practical Physics in SI, E Armitage (John Murray, 1981)

Study Notes for Technicians, J B Pratley (McGraw Hill, 1984)

Elements of Classical Physics, Martin and Hewett (Pergamon, 1975)

GCSE Physics, Nelkon and Detheridge (Pan Study Aid, 1987)

Advanced Physics, Tom Duncan (John Murray, 1981)

Higher Grade Physics, Stuart G Burns (English University Press, 1974)

Travel and Transport

	Engine	
aeroplane	+	
bicycle	−	
bus	+	
car	+	
coach	+	
helicopter	+	
lorry	+	
motorbike	+	
train	+	
van	+	

Contents and Index

Look through the following contents and index pages taken from *Office Skills* by Thelma J. Foster (Stanley Thornes, 1987) and try to find out where you could read about dictating machines.

Contents

Language Guidelines © 1990 ALBSU. Published by Hodder & Stoughton.

Index

Brickwork

Set out below are the titles of some chapters from *Brickwork 2* and the main headings from each of the chapters.
Under which chapter and main heading could you find the answer to the following questions?
If the answer was not under that heading, is there another heading which you could find it under?

1. What size gravel is used for pebble dashing?
   Chapter
   Main heading
   Other heading

2. What is a class II appliance?
   Chapter
   Main heading
   Other heading

3. What is the name given to a very small quadrant bend?
   Chapter
   Main heading
   Other heading

Chimneys and flues

Definitions – Structural requirements for chimneys – Construction of hearths – Fireplace recesses for Class I appliances – Flues and chimneys – Chimneys for Class I appliances – Flue linings – Chimney construction – Proximity of combustible material – Bonding for chimney stacks – Outlets of flues – Chimney pots – Damp prevention in chimney stacks – Self-assessment questions

Wall surface finishes

Fair-faced brickwork – Glazed bricks and tiles – Laying glazed bricks – Fixing glazed tiles – Glass blocks – Slate and tile hanging – Rendering external wall surfaces – Self-assessment questions

Drainage: clay products

Building Regulations – Glazed vitrified clay pipes – Joints – Types of fitting – Method of laying drains – Methods of laying vitrified stoneware drains – Testing drains – Inspection chambers – Intercepting chambers – Ventilation – Connecting a new drain to an existing drain – Clearing a blocked drain – Subsoil drains – Soakaways – Self-assessment questions

 Language Guidelines © 1990 ALBSU. Published by Hodder & Stoughton.

What happens to a cheque

When someone pays a cheque into their bank it is just the first step in a rather remarkable process. It is of no use just presenting a cheque to your bank, you need the value of the cheque credited to your bank account and to do this your bank must obtain the value of the cheque from the account of the drawer. This process is referred to as the clearing of cheques.

If you present to your bank a cheque drawn by someone who uses the same branch bank as you, then so long as the drawer has sufficient funds, the process is very simple. Your branch bank will transfer on paper the value of the cheque from the drawer's account to your account. If the drawer uses the same bank as you, but a different branch, the cheque will be sent to the Head Office of the bank and on to the branch of the drawer, and the value of the cheque will be sent in return.

Where the cheque presented is drawn by someone who uses a completely different bank the process is more complicated. The branch banks send the cheques of other banks to their own head office where they are sorted into piles of each of the other major banks they are drawn against. A representative of the bank takes the piles of cheques to the Clearing House.

At the Clearing House he meets the representatives of the other banks and gives them the cheques drawn on their banks and accepts cheques drawn on his bank. During this process an account is kept of the value of the piles of cheques changing hands and the difference between the value of the cheques received and handed over, shows how much each of the banks owes the others. This information is used daily to credit (add to) or debit (deduct from) the balances of the clearing banks which are kept at The Bank of England.

Note: A 'clearing bank' is a bank whose cheques are sorted through the London Bankers' Clearing House.

Look through the passage on 'Meat' and try to answer the question:
  'Collagen in the connective tissue is
      converted to _____ '
What are the key words to look for?
Underline them in the text.

Meat

Meat is probably the most important food that we use, accounting as it does for a major share of our total expenditure on food.

Cattle, sheep and pigs are reared for fresh meat and certain pigs are specifically produced for bacon. The animals are humanely killed and prepared in hygienic conditions, the skins or hides are removed, the innards are taken out of the carcass and the offal is put aside. The carcasses of beef are split into two sides and those of lambs, sheep, pigs and calves are left whole: they are then chilled in a cold room before being sent to market.

To cook meat properly it is necessary to know and understand the structure of meat. Lean flesh is composed of muscles, which are numerous bundles of fibres held together by connective tissue. The size of these fibres is extremely small, especially in tender cuts or cuts from young animals, and only the coarsest fibres may be distinguished by the naked eye. The size of the fibres varies in length, depth and thickness and this variation will affect the grain and the texture of the meat.

The quantity of connective tissue binding the fibres together will have much to do with the tenderness and eating quality. There are two kinds of connective tissue, the yellow (*elastin*) and the white (*collagen*). The thick yellow strip that runs along the neck and back of animals is an example of elastin. Elastin is found in the muscles, especially in older animals or those muscles receiving considerable exercise. Elastin will not cook, but it must be broken up mechanically by pounding or mincing. The white connective tissue collagen can be cooked, as it decomposes in moist heat to form gelatine. The amount of connective tissue in meat is determined by the age, breed, care and feed given to the animal.

The quantity of fat and its condition are important factors in determining eating quality. Fat is found on the exterior and interior of the carcass and in the flesh itself. Fat deposited between muscles or between the bundles of fibres is called marbling. If marbling is present, the meat is likely to be tender, of better flavour and moist. Much of the flavour of meat is given by fats found in lean or fatty tissues of the meat.

Gathering the news

a National newspapers also have reporters in important cities all over the world. They are known as *foreign correspondents*.

b A national newspaper will have about 50 full-time reporters. Every day, the news editor makes a list of events that are going to happen. He sends a reporter to each of them. The other reporters stay in the office, ready to collect information about unexpected events, such as fires, accidents or crimes.

c The chief news agency in Britain is the Press Association. It has more than 200 journalists. Every day, it sends out over 100 000 words from its offices in Fleet Street.

d A national newspaper gathers its news in three ways.

e A national newspaper will have about 2000 part-time reporters in towns all over Britain. These reporters are known as *local correspondents*. Most of them work full-time for a local or regional paper. When they have a story of general interest, they telephone a report to the national newspaper.

f Foreign news is supplied by agents like Reuters. This famous agency was founded in 1850 by a German called Reuter. He and his wife ran it, and at first they used pigeons to carry reports. Today, Reuters has 1100 correspondents in 183 different countries.

g Newspapers are also supplied with news by organisations called *news agencies*. A news agency has its own staff of reporters and correspondents. They send reports to the agency's offices. The news is then sent by a machine called a teleprinter to newspapers all over the country.

Language Guidelines © 1990 ALBSU. Published by Hodder & Stoughton.

Floppy disk

Using the list at the bottom of the page, write the names of the main components of a floppy disk.

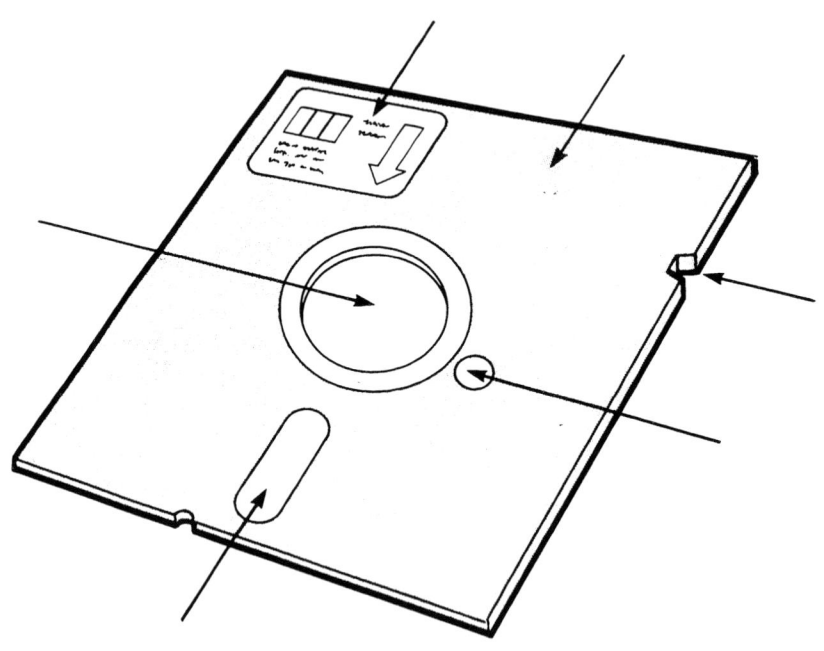

Label   Envelope   Write enable notch

Index hole   Read/Write window   Spindle hole

SCRIPT 1

Principle of Scanning

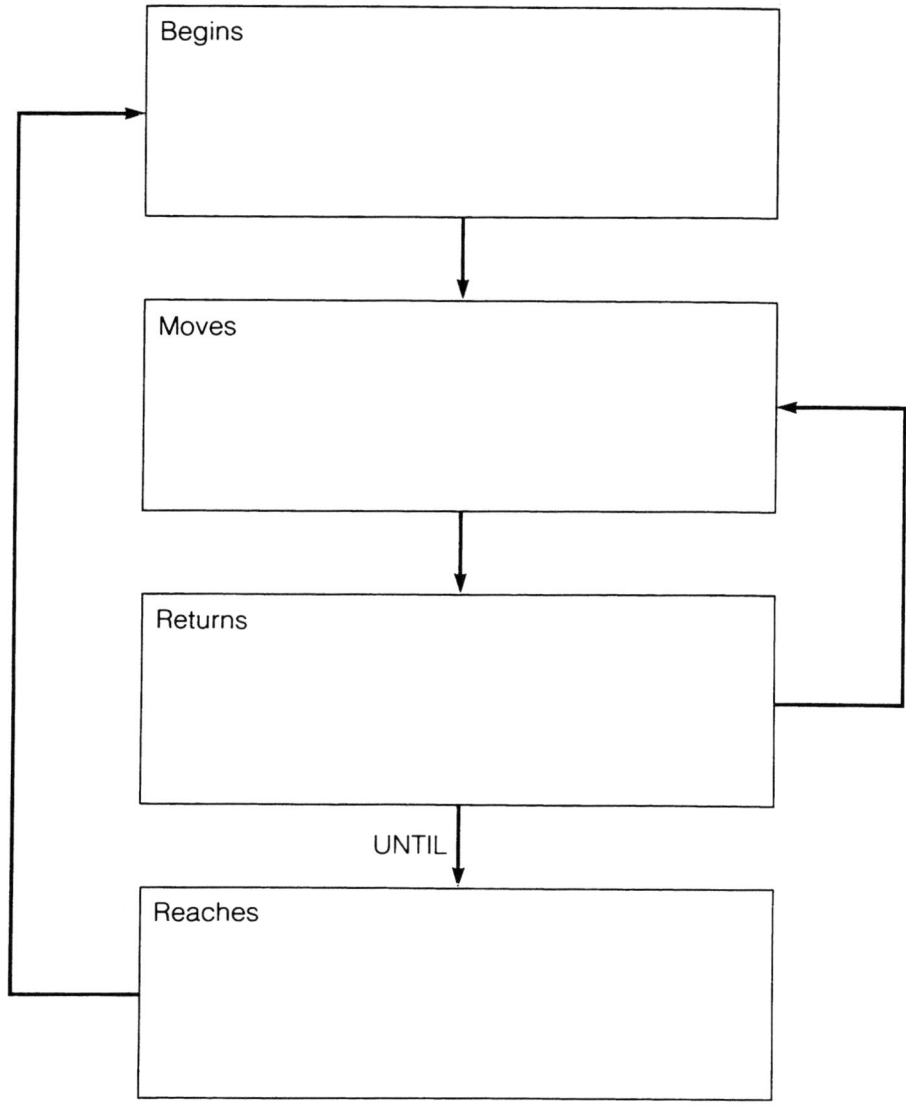

Begins

Moves

Returns

UNTIL

Reaches

SCRIPT 2

If you smell gas . . .

When you play the tape, you will hear a conversation about a gas leak. Some of the points they mention are listed below but others have been left out. Listen to what they say and fill in the missing points.

1. Put out cigarettes.

2.

3. Do not turn electrical switches on or off.

4.

5. Check if cooker and gas fire taps have been left on.

6. Check if pilot lights have gone out.

7.

8. Call the gas service.

SCRIPT 3

Fill in the chart.

Type of car	Shape	Number of doors	Number of passengers	Access to luggage space
Saloon				
Coupé				
Convertible				
Estate				
Hatchback				

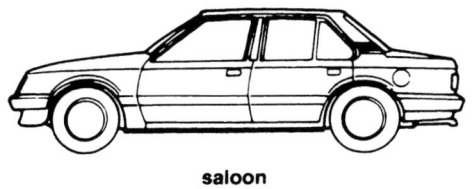

saloon

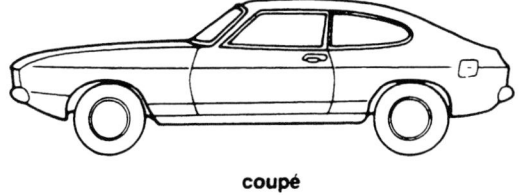

coupé

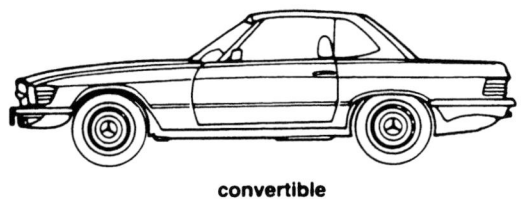

convertible

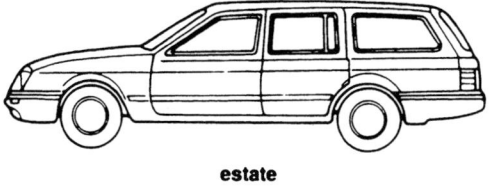

estate

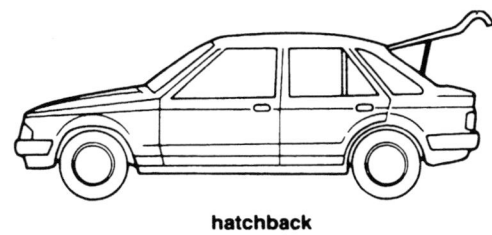

hatchback

SCRIPT 4

Reasons for the changes in agriculture

Pick out the correct answer to complete these statements.

1. Between 1800 and 1850, the population increased by

   a) 25%
   b) 50%
   c) 100%

2. People went to live in towns because

   a) houses were cheaper there
   b) the new industries needed workers
   c) food was cheaper there

3. Food could be delivered to the towns

   a) more quickly
   b) more cheaply
   c) more easily

4. Bread became dearer because

   a) coal was used to heat the ovens
   b) no corn was being imported from Europe
   c) the landowners needed more money to build their mansions

SCRIPT 5

Felt

Mark whether the following statements are true or false.

Felt is usually made from wool and other animal fibres.

True/False

Felt doesn't fray when it is cut.

True/False

Felt is suitable for making clothing.

True/False

Felt is hard wearing.

True/False

Felt is sometimes used for padding coats and jackets.

True/False

SCRIPT 6

Fastenings

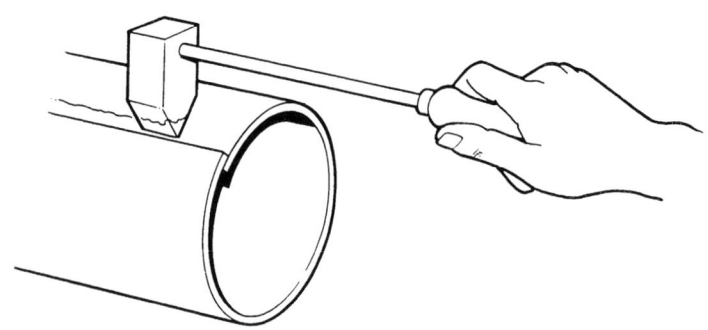

Make a list of as many different ways that you can think of for fastening engineering materials together. Against each one, write the advantages and disadvantages of using that particular method.

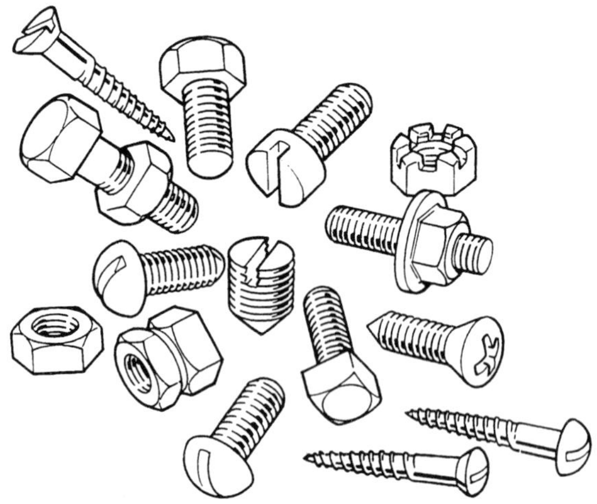

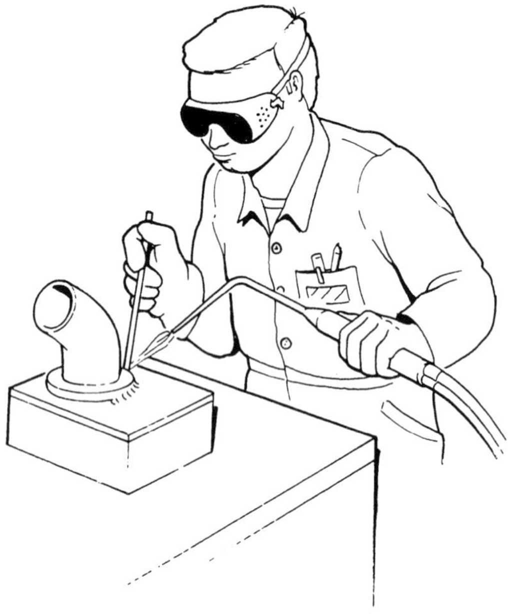

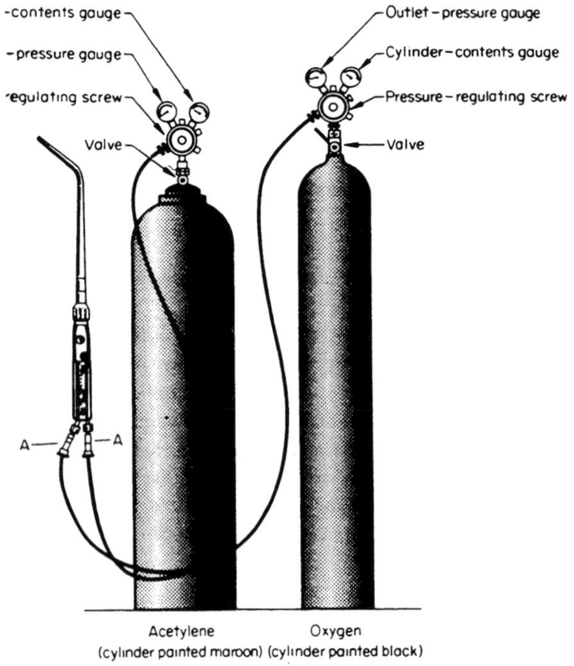

-contents gauge-

-pressure gauge-

regulating screw

Valve

Outlet – pressure gauge

Cylinder – contents gauge

Pressure – regulating screw

Valve

A——A

Acetylene
(cylinder painted maroon)

Oxygen
(cylinder painted black)

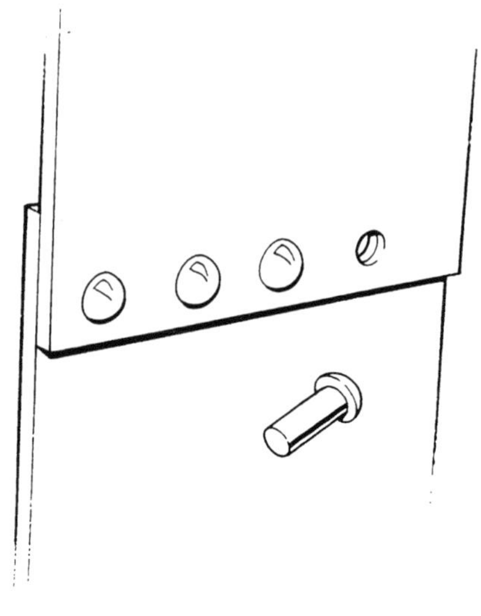

Look at the two pictures of motor cars. Make a list of all the changes that have taken place in design, technology and safety features. Some of the changes are labelled, but there are others. Then try to decide why these changes have taken place.

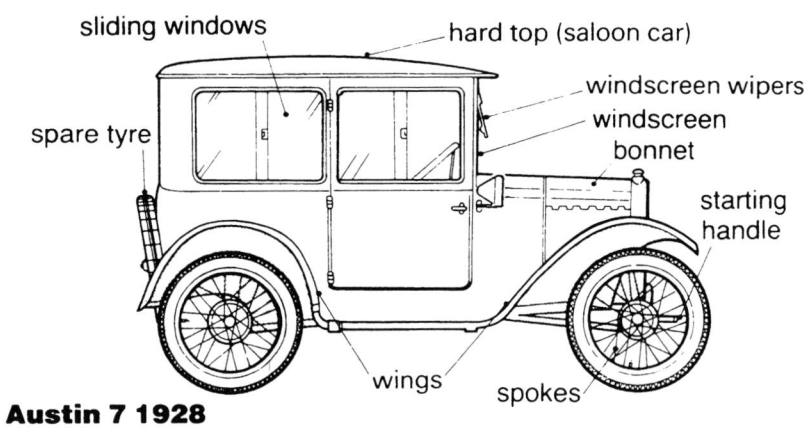

Austin 7 1928

sliding windows · hard top (saloon car) · windscreen wipers · windscreen · bonnet · spare tyre · starting handle · wings · spokes

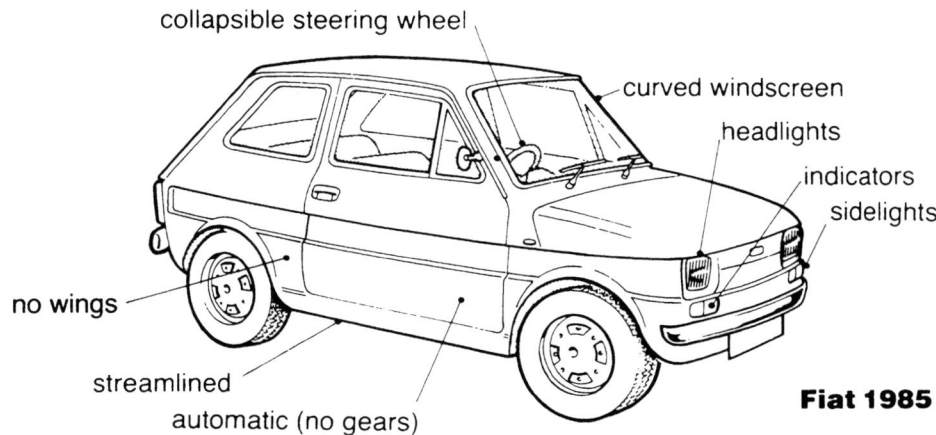

Fiat 1985

collapsible steering wheel · curved windscreen · headlights · indicators · sidelights · no wings · streamlined · automatic (no gears)

To make you think

Study this illustration carefully. List all the possible dangers in this kitchen.

When you have finished, suggest ways to make the kitchen safer.

Types of notes

Linear Notes

<u>Body typing</u> (somatyping)

(A) Endomorph
   i) Body pear shaped - wide at hips, narrow at shoulders
   ii) Head round
   iii) Fat on body, upper arms, thighs.
   iv) Slender at wrists, ankles.
   v) Wider front to back than side to side.

(B) Mesomorph
   i) Wedge shaped - wide at shoulders, narrow at hips.
   ii) Cubical massive head
   iii) Heavy, muscled arms, legs
   iv) Forearms, calves, strong relative to upper arms, thighs.
   v) Minimum amount of fat
   vi) Narrower front to back than side to side

(C) Ectomorph
   i) Narrow shoulders, hips
   ii) High peaked face, receding chin, high forehead
   iii) Thin chest, abdomen.
   iv) Spindly legs, arms
   v) Little muscle or fat
   vi) Large skin area, nervous system compared to size

Spidergram Notes

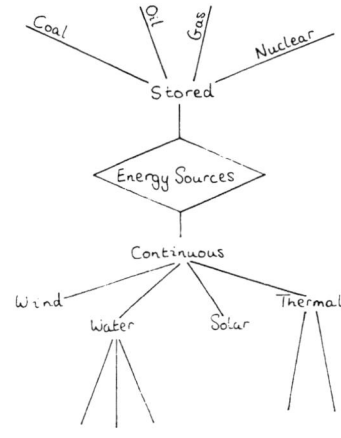

Different Energy Sources

Flow Charts

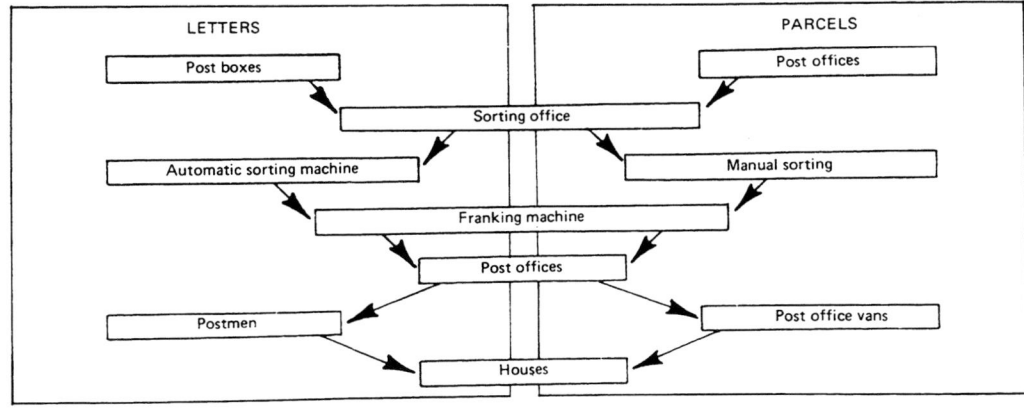

Letters and Parcels

Tabular Charts

Washer Removal for Shrouded Taps

ACTION	HOW	WHY
1. Prise up button in centre	plain tipped screwdriver	expose screw head
2. Undo screw	cross tipped screwdriver	release handle
3. Remove handle	pull up	explose gland nut
4. Unscrew gland nut	spanner or wrench	to remove head
5. Remove washer	*OLD TAPS* unscrew jumper nut *NEW TAPS* pull off jumper unit	

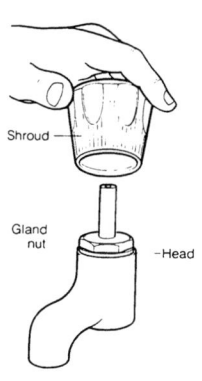

Maps

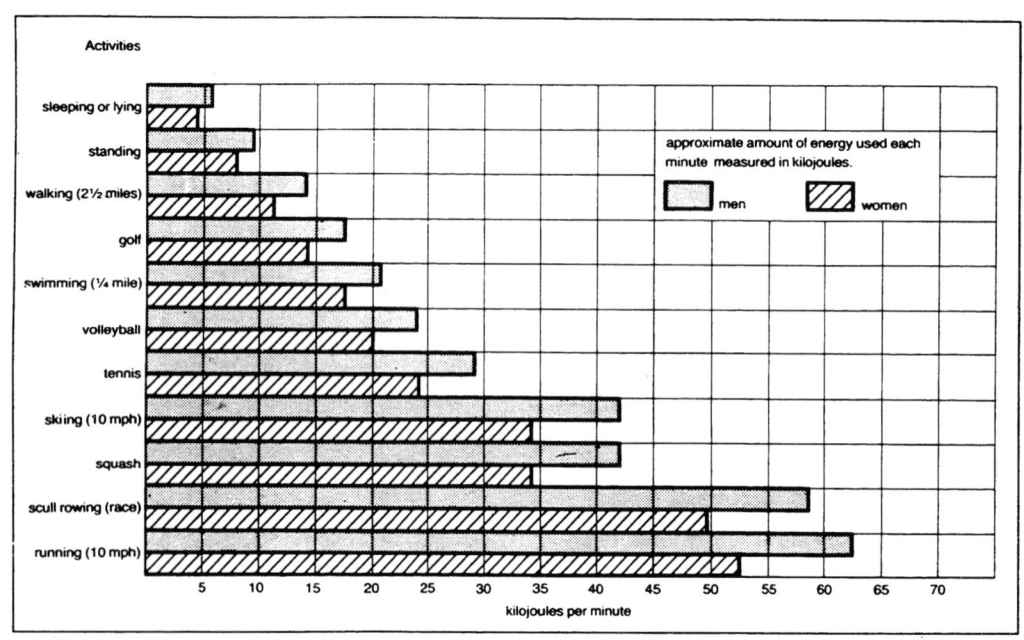

Scale:
0 100 200 km
0 50 100 150 miles

PRUSSIA

BATAVIAN
REPUBLIC
1798

1795
1795

R. Rhine

HOLY
ROMAN
EMPIRE

Vienna

Leoben

FRENCH
REPUBLIC

AUSTRIAN
POSSESSIONS

HELVETIC
REPUBLIC

SAVOY
1792

Milan

CISALPINE
REPUBLIC

VENETIA

Venice

1799
PIEDMONT

PARMA

Genoa

Bologna

1791

1793 Nice

LIGURIAN
REPUBLIC

Florence

TUSCANY

ROMAN
REP.

SPAIN

Corsica

Rome

PARTHENOPEAN
REPUBLIC

Sardinia

Naples

Annexed (with date)

French republic

French occupation

Sister republic

Diagrams

Object

Iris Ciliary Muscle

Cornea

Image on Retina

Aqueous
Humour

Optic Nerve
– to Brain

Crystalline Lens
(Changeable Thickness)

Object

Focus

Image
on Film

Camera
Lens

Iris Diaphragm

Graph

Light Intensity

100%

Daylight

Sunlight

Skylight

0.0

Dawn   Noon   Dusk

Time of Day ⟶

Bar Chart

Activities

sleeping or lying

standing

walking (2½ miles)

golf

swimming (¼ mile)

volleyball

tennis

skiing (10 mph)

squash

scull rowing (race)

running (10 mph)

approximate amount of energy used each
minute measured in kilojoules.

men   women

5   10   15   20   25   30   35   40   45   50   55   60   65   70

kilojoules per minute

The energy used in a variety of activities by a man of 65 kg and a woman of 55 kg

Language Guidelines © 1990 ALBSU. Published by Hodder & Stoughton.

Tree Diagram

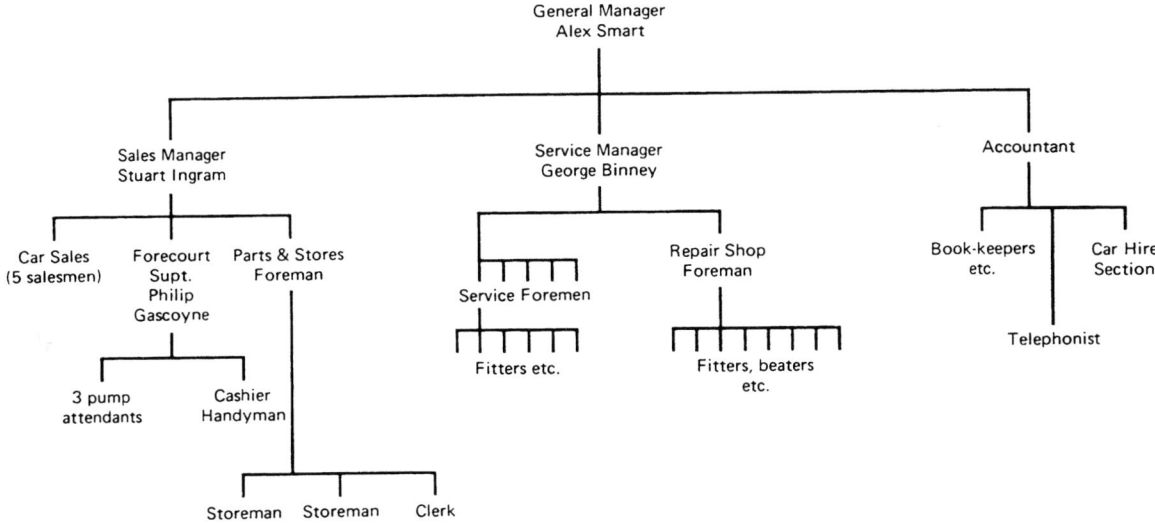

Pie Chart

The year's sales of a department store

Classifying

Linear Notes

Musical Instruments
① Played hands only
   a) keyboards
   b) string
   c) percussion
② Played hands and mouth
   a) brass
   b) woodwind

Spidergram notes

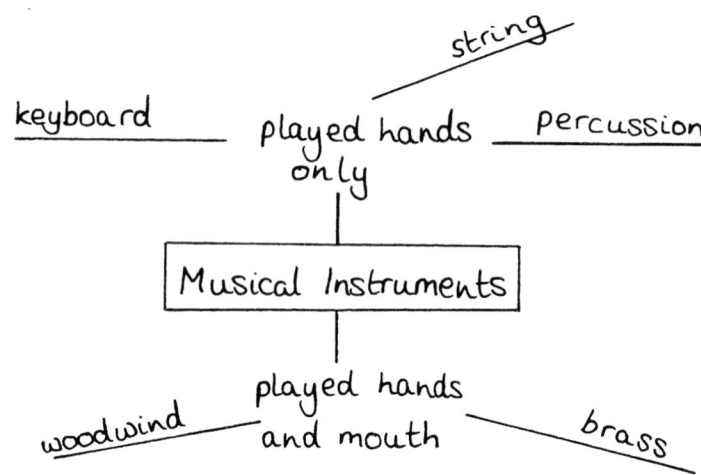

Tree diagram notes

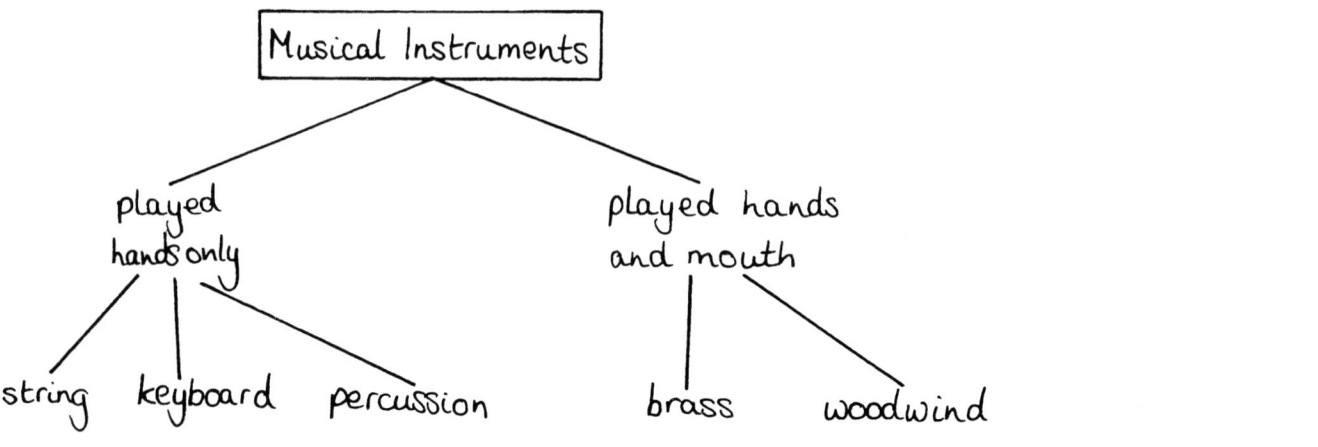

Language Guidelines © 1990 ALBSU. Published by Hodder & Stoughton.

DESCRIPTION OF PROCESS

Diagram

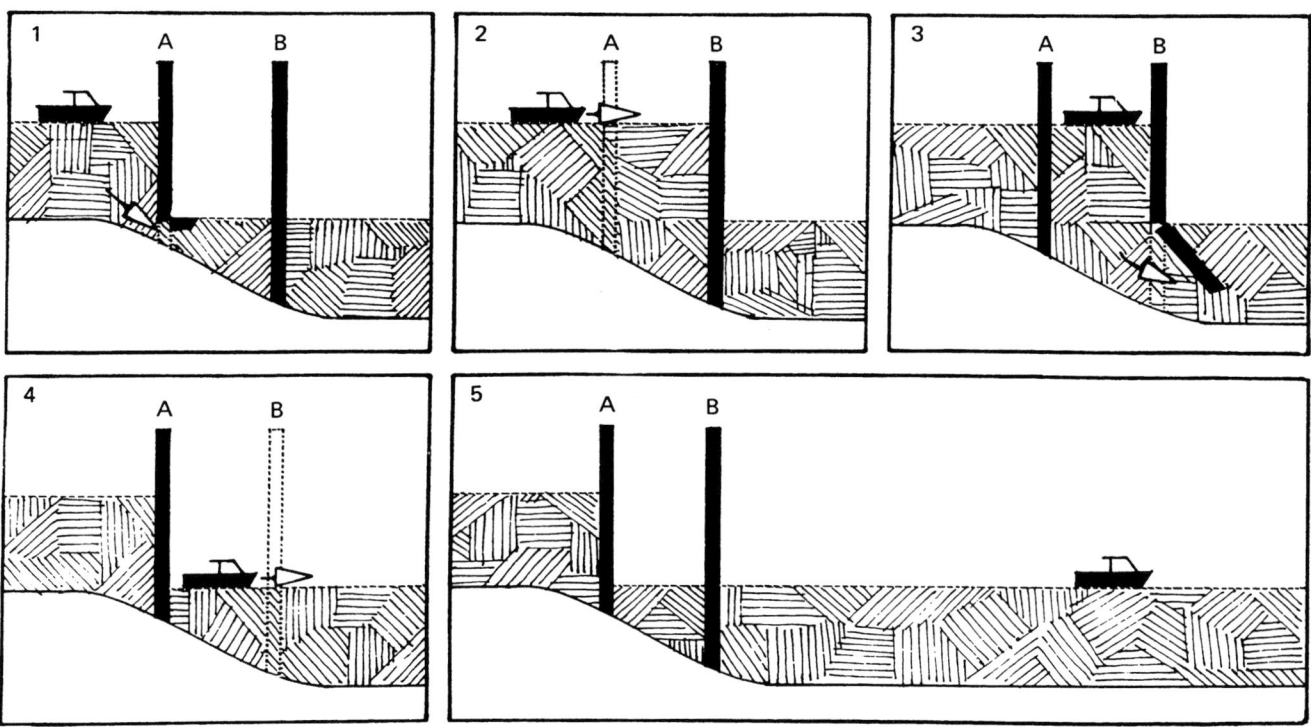

How a Lock Works

Tabular chart

	Item	Action	Place
1	Paddle	opened	in first gate
2	Water	rises	in lock
3	First gate	opened	
4	Boat	enters	lock
5	First gate	closed	
6	Paddle	opened	in second gate
7	Water	drops	in lock
8	Second gate	opened	
9	Boat	leaves	lock
10	Second gate	closed	

Abbreviations

We can use abbreviations to make notes more quickly.
You must decide
a) *which* words to abbreviate.
b) *how* to abbreviate them. You should use the shortest abbreviation which will make sense when you read it back.

Invent your own abbreviations for the following words:

hour
week
arithmetic
modern
between
preparation
very
especially
black and white
would
consistency

What do you think the following abbreviations mean?

dest
exct
acc.
min.
diff.
soc.
prob.
shd
pt
exp.
cont.
rem.

Language Guidelines © 1990 ALBSU. Published by Hodder & Stoughton.

Look at the photographs and match them to these place names:

Lake Mead, Las Vegas, Hoover Dam, Grand Canyon, Imperial Valley, Monument Valley.

Colorado River

Look carefully at the map and then fill in the blank spaces in the sentences.

The Colorado River rises high in the _____ mountains. Hundreds of mountain streams flow into it gathering water from the melting _____ and rainfall in the mountains. After crossing the deserts of _____ the river flows into Lake _____ . Near here there are spectacular rock formations in _____ Valley. The Colorado has cut a hugh gorge in the plateau lands of _____ . It is called the _____ . Further downstream there is a big dam across the river. It is the _____ Dam and holds back the water forming Lake _____ . People come here from the town of L_____ V_____ only half an hour's drive away. Water sports like _____ are popular in the hot, desert climate. Some of the river water is sent to Los _____ by _____ for city water supply. Further downstream its waters are sent into the irrigation channels of _____ valley for the fruit orchards there. Only a trickle of water reaches the country of _____ .

Worksheet for extended activities.

Try to answer the following questions from what you already know. If you cannot answer a question, go to the library and look for the information.

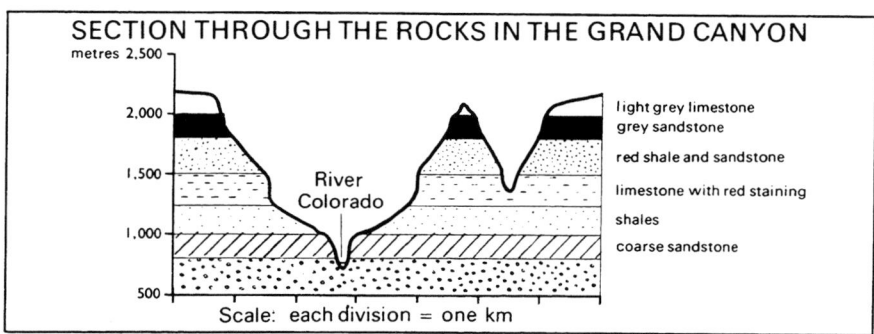

SECTION THROUGH THE ROCKS IN THE GRAND CANYON

metres 2,500

2,000

1,500

River
Colorado

1,000

500

Scale: each division = one km

light grey limestone
grey sandstone

red shale and sandstone

limestone with red staining

shales

coarse sandstone

Look at the diagram of the Grand Canyon. How far is it from one rim of the gorge to the opposite side? How far is it from the top plateau to the bed of the river?

Hollywood is near Los Angeles. What made Hollywood famous and why was its location chosen?

There are huge aircraft industries in California. Suggest why the climate is suitable for this.

The Colorado River provides the water for several large cities. Where does our town get its water supply from?

How will your interview end?

Handout for role play

DON'T
– Smoke
– Interrupt
– Just answer 'Yes' or 'No'
– Swear . . . even mildly
– Argue
– Be personal or familiar
– Be cocky
– Interview the interviewer
– Criticise your past employers
– Ask about wages until the last possible moment

DO
– Think of each interview as a practice
– Be early . . . about 5–10 minutes
– Be neat and tidy
– Knock confidently and walk in
– Smile
– Sit back comfortably in your chair
– Pause and think before answering
– Speak clearly
– Be enthusiastic
– Stick to the point
– Be truthful and sincere
– Ask the interviewer some questions about the job
– Look at the interviewer and listen carefully
– Thank the interviewer for seeing you
– Remember you are being assessed from the minute you walk into the building . . . be polite to the receptionist and other staff

Language Guidelines © 1990 ALBSU. Published by Hodder & Stoughton.

Handout for role play

NUCLEAR POWER

Why We Need Nuclear Energy

* Nuclear power stations have proved safe, clean, reliable and economic. The electricity boards calculate that electricity generated by nuclear power costs less to produce than electricity generated by burning coal, and much less than electricity generated by burning oil.
* Oil and coal are limited resources. As nuclear energy expands its contribution to electricity production, it will allow coal to substitute for oil where possible. The use of oil can then be concentrated on those areas where there is no substitute possible, e.g. air transport.

1. The situation
There are plans to build a nuclear power station near your town. The town council has arranged a public meeting to discuss the issue.

2. Groups at the meeting
■ Chairman of the town council
■ Members of the public
■ Representatives of the Anti-Nuclear Action Group (ANAG)
■ Representatives of the Nuclear Energy Authority (NEA)
■ Reporters from the local newspapers are also present.

3. Agenda for the meeting
1) The chairman explains why the meeting has been called and introduces the representatives of the NEA and ANAG.
2) The NEA and ANAG explain their points of view (3 minutes each).
3) Members of the public and reporters ask questions (10 minutes).
4) The NEA and the ANAG sum up (2 minutes each).
5) The chairman asks everyone at the meeting except the reporters to vote for or against the nuclear power station.

4. Instructions

■ Chairman of the town council
Draw a map showing where the nuclear power station will be. You should get as many members of the public as possible to ask questions.

■ Members of the public
Make a list of questions you want to ask. Think about:
unemployment   cost   safety
Discuss the planned nuclear power station with the other members of the public before the meeting starts.

■ Representatives of the Anti-Nuclear Action Group
Read through *Nuclear Power, No Thanks*. Think about costs and safety. What problems may a nuclear power station cause your town? How will the NEA dispose of the radioactive waste from the power station?

■ Representatives of the Nuclear Energy Authority
Read through *Why We Need Nuclear Energy*. Your position is very simple: the country needs more energy and nuclear power is cheap and efficient. A survey has shown that the best site for a nuclear power station is near the town. Building the power station will take many years and provide a large number of jobs.
    Think of as many arguments for the nuclear power station as possible.

■ Reporters from the local newspapers
Listen to the discussion and take notes. Then use your notes to write a report for your wall newspaper. While the groups are preparing you can interview the Chairman, or try to think of possible headlines. You do not speak in the discussion or vote, but you can ask questions.

NUCLEAR POWER? NO THANKS

Q: Do we need nuclear power?
A: No, because the world has reserves of coal which will last for hundreds of years. We should invest in research into renewable energy sources like solar power, wind power and the use of power from tides and waves.
Q: Would jobs be lost if nuclear power was abandoned?
A: No. More jobs would be available. Nuclear reactors absorb huge amounts of money which, if spent on other energy projects, would create far more jobs. It costs £2 million to create a job in a nuclear power station.
Q: Is nuclear power the cheapest energy available?
A: No. It turns out to be the most expensive. If the true costs are counted, such as the large numbers of reactor failures and research into the problem of nuclear waste disposal, it turns out to be very expensive.

THE FLOPPY DISK

Right, now if you can all look this way a minute, I'll just explain some of the features of a floppy disk and then I'll hand them round and you can all have a go at loading one into your disk drive. You should all have a sheet with a diagram of a floppy disk on and you can label the parts as we go along. Is there anyone who hasn't got a sheet? Right.

As you can see, the disk itself is kept inside this paper envelope which protects it and makes sure that it doesn't get damaged or marked by grubby fingers. However, so that the computer can read or write things on the disk, there are a few holes or windows cut in the paper envelope. This oblong one at the bottom here is the read/write window and this smaller, circular one at the side is the index hole. The big hole in the middle is the spindle hole which acts like the hole in the middle of a record and centres the disk in the disk drive. On the right hand side here, a small piece has been cut out of the envelope. This is the write enable notch and if this were missing or you covered it up with a piece of sticky paper or something, you would not be able to put anything new onto the disk. Finally, the label at the top left hand corner is used to show the title of the programs on the disk.

Right. Any questions? Have you all managed to label your diagrams? O.K. I'll hand these round and we can go onto how the disk is loaded into the disk drive.

TASK SHEET: 23

THE PRINCIPLE OF SCANNING

To produce a picture on a television screen, an electron beam is projected onto the screen creating a small spot of light. By passing a suitable electric current through several deflector coils, the beam can be moved and so the spot of light will move across and down the screen.

Initially, the spot of light is positioned in the top left hand corner of the screen as viewed from the front. It then moves very rapidly across the screen horizontally until it reaches the other side. The spot then returns to the left hand side of the screen, again very rapidly, but this time it is positioned below the point where it had initially started from. This rapid return is called the fly-back.

A second line is now traced by moving the spot of light horizontally across the screen and again when the spot reaches the other side, it returns very rapidly to the left hand side of the screen slightly below the line it has just traced.

This process is repeated until the spot of light finally reaches the bottom right hand corner of the screen which means that a complete picture has been traced. The spot of light now returns to the top left hand corner of the screen and the whole process is repeated.

If the process is repeated so that more than sixteen pictures per second are traced and the intensity of the spot remains constant, then the screen appears to be a complete white picture or raster.

TASK SHEET: 24

3 IF YOU SMELL GAS . . .

A: John. John. Can you come here a minute? I'm sure I can smell gas.

B: What?

A: I said I think I can smell gas here in the kitchen.

B: O.K. I'm coming . . . oops. Better put this cigarette out first. Now, where can you smell gas?

A: Over here by the cooker. I'll just see if it's working.

B: Don't.

A: What?

B: Don't strike any matches. You could blow us up. If you think you can smell gas, you mustn't use matches or a naked flame. And don't turn on any electrical switches.

A: Why not?

B: If you turn a switch on or off, it can make a spark which could ignite the gas.

A: I hadn't thought of that.

B: Yes. Well. I think you're right about the smell of gas. We'd better open the doors and windows to get rid of any gas that's built up in the room.

A: This window's stuck. I told you to be careful the last time you painted it. Now it's all gummed up and I can't get it open. Ah! That's done it.

B: Have you checked that all the cooker taps are off?

A: Yes. They're all off.

B: What about the fire?

A: No. I didn't check that. The gas seemed to be coming from round the cooker.

B: Well, better check it just to be sure.

A: No. It's not on.

B: What about the pilot light on the boiler? Is it still on?

A: Yes. It seems to be.

B: Then there must be a leak somewhere. We'd better turn off the supply.

A: How do we do that?

B: There's a tap next to the gas meter. Can you turn it off while I call the gas service?

A: O.K. I'll go down.

B: Don't! Stop!

A: What?

B: Don't turn on any switches.

A: Oh, yes. Sorry. I forgot. It's a bit dark down here but I think . . .

TASK SHEET: 25

TYPES OF MOTOR VEHICLE

Cars are classified by the body, shape, number of passengers and the number or type of doors. The main types are:

- The *saloon* is a covered two or four doored car for four to eight people. This shape is based on three boxes, the front box is the engine compartment, followed by the passenger space and the luggage space. The three sections are then blended together to produce a pleasing appearance.

- The *coupé* versions are normally two door models intended for two people, the driver and one other. These still conform to the three box layout but access to the luggage space may be by means of a tailgate. Also some versions are classed as 2+2 models, which means the rear seat is rather cramped for adults but is suitable for children or for occasional adult use.

- The *convertible* car has two doors and can be turned into an open car by either removing or lowering the roof. They normally carry four passengers, with the luggage and engine in separate compartments.

- An *estate* car normally has an extended roof to provide large internal luggage space. A tailgate enables bulky or long objects to be loaded. Therefore the car only requires a separate compartment for the engine. There are normally seats for four passengers and may be either two or four doored.

- The *hatchback* models are half-way between a saloon and an estate car. By including the tailgate as one door the car is made in three and five door versions. Normally seats for four passengers are provided. As the roof is extended to the rear of the vehicle, the only other compartment required is for the engine. Although it is built on the three box shape, the large rear door means it is similar to an estate car.

TASK SHEET: 26

THE REASONS FOR THE CHANGES IN AGRICULTURE

The reasons for the changes in agriculture during the eighteenth and nineteenth centuries can only be fully understood if we look at some of the other developments that were taking place in Britain at about this time.

One of the major changes was the rapid increase in the population which of course meant that there was a need for more food to be produced. The number of people in England and Wales increased by about 50 per cent between 1750 and 1800 and then doubled between 1800 and 1850. The old system of farming had only just been sufficient to feed everyone in 1700 and yet by 1850 the demand for food had trebled. So it was not surprising that even with the changes in farming methods, there were many people who went hungry, particularly among the poor.

Another change that occurred about this time was the rapid growth of the industrial towns as people moved away from the country to find jobs in the new industries. Previously, most people had a small plot of land where they were able to grow some of their food but when they moved to the towns, they had to rely entirely on the farmer for their food.

Fortunately, at the same time, there was a

rapid improvement in travel and transport. Better roads, and later the railways, made it easier to take food from the country to the towns and also deliver the coal and new machinery that the farmers needed.

The Revolutionary and Napoleonic wars which lasted from 1793 to 1815 meant that European corn couldn't be imported. As a result grain was scarce and consequently prices went up steeply. The rise in prices gave the farmers a larger profit from what they grew and so encouraged them to produce more food from their land.

Finally, people who had previously made money from trade now built large mansions and applied their business skills to the running of their estates. They could now see that it was possible to make money from farming.

TASK SHEET: 27

SCRIPT 6 — THE ADVANTAGES AND DISADVANTAGES OF FELT

Wool and some other animal fibres have a natural tendency to mat together when they are moistened, heated and then put under mechanical pressure. In this way, the fibres are consolidated together into a fabric which has no grain since the fibres are pointing in all directions.

It's because of this that you can cut felt in any direction and it won't fray or unravel. That's its main advantage, but unfortunately the structure of felt also means that it does have some disadvantages which make it unsuitable for normal garment making.

To make felt strong and stable, the fibres have to be consolidated in such a way that the felt is stiff and heavy so that it doesn't drape very well. But if the felt is made so that it is soft and supple, then it is not strong or hard wearing. So felt isn't used much for making clothes. It is used for making hats, where its capacity to be shaped by heat and moisture can be exploited and it's also used for applique work where intricate shapes need to be cut without the fabric fraying. Certain types of felt are also used for padding garment interlinings.

TASK SHEET: 28

SCRIPT 7 — CHEQUES

A cheque is an order to your bank to pay a stated sum of money to the bearer of that cheque or the person named on the cheque. Today it is usual for cheques to be written on forms printed by the banks, though there is nothing to stop you writing a cheque on a piece of paper. There have been examples of cheques being written on more unusual materials, such as a cow, which is still perfectly legal, though I would think it wasn't very convenient.

All cheques have the name of the bank and the address of the branch where it is to be drawn. This is the branch where your account is. This bank is known as the drawee. In the top right hand corner and again at the bottom, there will be a branch code number. This is usually written out in magnetic characters to make it easier for sorting by machine.

In the bottom left hand corner is the cheque number which is also written out in magnetic characters. The bank keeps a record of the cheque numbers so that they can debit the money from the right customer's account. This cheque number will also appear on the customer's statement so that they can check that all their cheques have been debited correctly.

Also at the bottom is the customer's account number. Every customer has their own number and this appears on all their cheques, paying-in slips and statements. Very often, nowadays, the customer's name will also be printed on the cheque just above the space for the signature.

Those are the usual things that are already printed on a cheque. Now we'll look at the things that have to be written on the cheque by the customer. The first thing, at the top, is the date when the cheque is written. It is possible to write a later date on the cheque so that it cannot be drawn immediately but banks do not encourage it. This is called post-dating a cheque. A cheque is not valid six months after the date written at the top.

The next thing which has to be written on is the name of the person to whom the cheque is being given. This person, or it may be a company, is called the payee. This is written on the line below the name of the bank.

On the next two lines below this are written the amount of money that is to be payed. The amount of pounds has to be written out in words then you put a dash and the amount of pence can be written in numbers. If there are no pence, that is, the amount is a whole number of pounds, then you write 'only' after you have written the amount of pounds. This is to stop anyone adding a few pence after you have written the cheque.

On the right of these two lines is a small box in which the amount that has to be paid is then written out in numbers. It is important to check that the amount written in words agrees with that written in numbers, otherwise the bank will refuse to accept the cheque.

Finally, below this box, the customer must sign the cheque. If the customer does not sign the cheque or the signature is different from the specimen signature held at the bank, then the bank will refuse to accept the cheque.

SCRIPT 8 THE ROLE OF LOCAL COUNCILS IN LEISURE AND RECREATION

The main providers of recreation and sports facilities in this country are the local councils. Of course, the range of facilities will vary from place to place, but, taking the country as a whole, the councils provide more funding than any other body.

Almost a third of expenditure on leisure and recreation goes on the upkeep of parks and open spaces. The councils also provide many of the pitches for local football, cricket, tennis, golf and many other outdoor sports. Over the past 25 years more indoor leisure centres have been built from council funds to provide for a host of

sports activities such as badminton, squash, weight training and basket ball. The councils are usually responsible for swimming pools and swimming is the most popular indoor sport in this country.

But the council don't spend all their money on sports facilities. In 1983–4, the councils in England and Wales spent £47 million on community halls and public halls, which are used for a vast range of local neighbourhood recreational activities. The local councils also provide youth clubs either individually or in conjunction with a national youth organisation.

It has been estimated that 70 per cent of all boys and 60 per cent of all girls between the ages of 14 and 20 attend a youth club of some kind.

The majority of the country's art galleries and museums are run by the local council and in the year 1984–5 they spent £150 million. The council also run the local libraries of which there are 5,395 in the United Kingdom, which hold a stock of approximately 140 million books.

The local councils also help to support local theatres and concert halls and often give grants to local theatre groups and music groups. In 1983–4 this amounted to £66 million pounds.

SCRIPT 9 A DAY IN THE LIFE . . .

Reporter: Today, I've come to a large riding stables in the heart of Wiltshire, and standing here beside me I have the head girl of the stables, Judy Gresham. Apart from looking after horses, the stables also train students for the BHS examination so Judy is kept very busy dividing her time between the horses, the clients of the stables and the students. Can you describe a typical day for me, Judy?

Judy: Yes. Well, we usually start at about 7.30 when we prepare the morning feed for all the horses. This is usually done by the students, but as some of the livery horses have special diets, I have to supervise so that they get the right feed.

Reporter: What do you mean by livery horses, Judy?

Judy: These are the horses that are owned by someone else and we just provide the stabling for them and make sure that they are exercised and kept fit.

Reporter: Ah, yes. What do you do next?

Judy: At about 8.00 the students feed the horses and muck out. Again, my job is to supervise and make sure that they do this properly. After this, we have our breakfasts at about 9.00 and after breakfast the students groom the horses and prepare them and themselves for their riding lesson. While they're doing this, I usually spend my time checking any of the horses which have been injured or are sick.

Reporter: Do you get a lot of problems?

Judy: No. We've been fairly fortunate so far, touch wood, and we haven't had anything serious. Though you always get the horse who has an odd knock now and again.

Reporter: I suppose you have the riding lessons next?

Judy: Yes. At about 11.00 the students have an hour's lesson and then, when they return to the yard, they brush the horses off and give them their mid-day feed. Lunch is about 1.00 but before this we tidy up the yard. After lunch, I take the students for an hour's lesson on stable management and teaching practice and then at 3.00 they spend about an hour cleaning the tack. Then at about 4.00 we start to get ready to bed the horses for the night although some of them might have to be prepared for an evening session in the summer.

Reporter: I suppose that whilst you're doing all this you have lots of other things that crop up?

Judy: Yes. We always have clients calling to check on their horses or wanting to go out for a ride and the weekends can be particularly hectic. Then there's the feed and things to organise and make sure that we have enough in.

Reporter: But your day finishes at about 5.00 then, does it?

Judy: Oh no. I like to check all the horses last thing at night and of course, living on the job means that we can be called out at any time if a horse is sick or someone wants to discuss something about the stabling of their horse.

Reporter: Well, thank you, Judy. I don't know whether that has put off any would-be stable girls but it certainly sounds an interesting and varied life.

KEYPOINT QUESTIONS

Narrative
- Who were the people involved?
- Where did things happen?
- What were they trying to achieve – what were their overall objectives?
- Were there any obstacles or problems they had to overcome?
- What were the different ways in which they tried to overcome these problems?
- Did they base their ideas on any work carried out by other people?
- Were there any failures?
- Why did they fail?
- How long did particular events or actions last?
- Are there any important dates?
- What were the eventual outcomes?

Description of structure or mechanism
- What shape is it?
- What size is it?
- What colour is it?
- Where would you find it?
- Is there a reason for its location?
- What are the constituent parts?
- Where are these parts located?
- What materials is it made of?
- What is it used for?
- How does it work?
- How is it powered?
- What effect does it have – what changes take place?
- How long will it last?
- Are there any identifiable features?

Description of process
- What are the different stages of the process?
- What order do they happen in?
- What action occurs during each stage?
- How often do things happen?
- How long does each action last?
- How does what happens to one thing affect what happens to another?
- What pieces of machinery are used?
- Who are the people involved and what do they do?

- Are there any relevant times or dates?
- What is the original state of the product?
- Are there any by-products?

Instruction
- In what order should things be done?
- What pieces of equipment or machinery should be used?
- What part of a machine or piece of equipment should be used?
- Is there a special reason why certain things have to be done?
- How long do you need to do something for?
- What measurements need to be made or taken?
- What should the eventual outcome be?
- Are there any precautions that need to be taken?

Classification
- What is the main group called?
- What are the different sub-groups called?
- What are the criteria for any of the groups?

Cause/Effect
- What are the causes?
- What effect did they have?
- How did that effect come about?
- How long did it take?

Exemplifying
- What is the general principle or rule?
- Are there any examples or evidence of how it applies?
- Are there any advantages in its application?
- Are there any disadvantages in its application?
- How are the disadvantages overcome?
- Are there any exceptions to the general principle or rule?

Advantages/Disadvantages
- What are the advantages?
- What are the disadvantages?

Language Guidelines © 1990 ALBSU. Published by Hodder & Stoughton.